PRAYER - MEETING METHODS

HOW TO PREPARE FOR AND
CONDUCT CHRISTIAN
ENDEAVOR PRAYER MEETINGS
AND SIMILAR GATHERINGS

BY
AMOS R. WELLS

MANAGING EDITOR OF THE GOLDEN RULE,
AND AUTHOR OF "SOCIAL EVENINGS," "THE
JUNIOR MANUAL," "WAYS OF WORKING
SERIES," "FOREMAN JENNIE," ETC.

First Fruits Press
Wilmore, Kentucky
c2015

Prayer-meeting methods : how to prepare for and conduct Christian endeavor prayer meetings and similar gatherings, by Amos R. Wells.

First Fruits Press, ©2015
Previously published: Boston and Chicago: United Society of Christian Endeavor, ©1916.

ISBN: 9781621713845 (print), 9781621713852 (digital)

Digital version at http://place.asburyseminary.edu/christianendeavorbooks/19/

First Fruits Press is a digital imprint of the Asbury Theological Seminary, B.L. Fisher Library. Asbury Theological Seminary is the legal owner of the material previously published by the Pentecostal Publishing Co. and reserves the right to release new editions of this material as well as new material produced by Asbury Theological Seminary. Its publications are available for noncommercial and educational uses, such as research, teaching and private study. First Fruits Press has licensed the digital version of this work under the Creative Commons Attribution Noncommercial 3.0 United States License. To view a copy of this license, visit http://creativecommons.org/licenses/by-nc/3.0/us/.

For all other uses, contact:

First Fruits Press
B.L. Fisher Library
Asbury Theological Seminary
204 N. Lexington Ave.
Wilmore, KY 40390
http://place.asburyseminary.edu/firstfruits

Wells, Amos R. (Amos Russel), 1862-1933.
    Prayer-meeting methods : how to prepare for and conduct Christian endeavor prayer meetings and similar gatherings / by Amos R. Wells.
    184 pages ; 21 cm.
    Wilmore, Ky. : First Fruits Press, ©2015.
    On cover: A book of plans for young people's religious gatherings.
    Reprint. Previously published: Boston : United Society of Christian Endeavor, ©1916.
    ISBN: 9781621713845 (pbk.)
    1. Prayer meetings I. Title.
BV285 .W4 2015

Cover design by Jonathan Ramsay

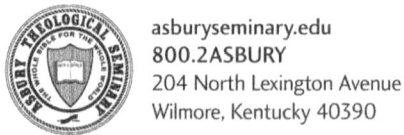

First Fruits Press
The Academic Open Press of Asbury Theological Seminary
204 N. Lexington Ave., Wilmore, KY 40390
859-858-2236
first.fruits@asburyseminary.edu
asbury.to/firstfruits

PRAYER-MEETING METHODS

HOW TO PREPARE FOR AND CONDUCT

CHRISTIAN ENDEAVOR PRAYER MEETINGS

AND SIMILAR GATHERINGS

BY

AMOS R. WELLS

MANAGING EDITOR OF "THE GOLDEN RULE," AND AUTHOR OF
"SOCIAL EVENINGS," "THE JUNIOR MANUAL,"
"WAYS OF WORKING SERIES,"
"FOREMAN JENNIE,"
ETC.

———

BOSTON AND CHICAGO
UNITED SOCIETY OF CHRISTIAN ENDEAVOR

COPYRIGHT, 1896, 1916,

BY THE

UNITED SOCIETY OF CHRISTIAN ENDEAVOR.

All rights reserved

CONTENTS.

CHAPTER		PAGE
I.	Taking Part in the Meeting	5
II.	The General Work of the Committee	20
III.	The Committee and the Society	39
IV.	The Committee and the Church	46
V.	At Home	53
VI.	The Leader	62
VII.	Prayer in the Meetings	83
VIII.	Using the Bible	92
IX.	Emphasize the Pledge	100
X.	The Music	107
XI.	Points for Good Meetings	114
XII.	Special Meetings	130
XIII.	The Topic Cards	159
XIV.	Some Closing Suggestions	167
XV.	A Budget of Fresh Methods	175

PRAYER-MEETING METHODS.

CHAPTER I.

TAKING PART IN THE MEETING.

HAVE you ever heard any one say, "I cannot express myself"? That is true only of an idiot or a paralytic. Not express yourself? Why, if you were born dumb, still eyes can speak lovingly, and helpful hands can pronounce beautiful orations. If you are blind and deaf, yet you can point to heaven. If you are helpless and motionless, still they preach noble sermons who only stand and wait.

Self Always Expresses Itself.

But those who say, "I cannot express myself," do not usually mean that they cannot express themselves at all. They mean that they cannot express themselves fully, but only stammeringly and inadequately.

But this also is untrue. Self always expresses itself. If you think you cannot express all of yourself, then you are mistaken in one of two ways. Either you are already expressing more of yourself than you know, or you may think you have a larger self to express than you really have.

Be assured that you cannot hide spiritual heat and spiritual light, any more than you can hide physical heat and physical light. If the love of mankind, if the spirit of prayer and of praise, could lurk unobserved in the human heart, then I could believe in an expressionless heaven, where harpstrings vibrate without sound, and the glory of God shines without giving light.

But no. The stammering soul speaks stammeringly, however glib the tongue. The steadfast spirit talks steadfastly, in spite, often, of faltering speech. It would be sad indeed if this were not true.

The Value of Words.

Suppose, however, we merely say, "I cannot express myself in words." What then? Well, this too is false; and to prove that it is false is my present purpose. I shall try, first, to show the value of verbal expression; and second, to show how we can win this power.

In the first place, then, why is it that Paul says that "with the mouth confession is made unto salvation"? Are not the issues of life out of the heart? Why is it that Christians always insist on verbal expression of religious feeling? I will mention eight reasons.

Earnestness Means Expression.

First, because, when we are in earnest about anything else, speech is so common and ready. Young people proclaim zealously, "I want to go to that party"; "I love ice cream"; "John is helping me level the tennis-court." Why should they stammer and break down when they say, "I want to go to heaven"; "I love the Saviour"; "Christ is helping me live a manly life"? The sceptic will have it that this hesitancy argues more love for ice cream than for Christ.

No Mistake About It.

In the second place, verbal expression is valuable because it is so unmistakable. "What!" you cry, "are there none whose professions are only loud-voiced shams?" Yes; but whom do these deceive? Can you not detect their insincerity almost with the first word?

It is much easier to be deceived by looks than by speech. Yonder pretty girl, with serious eyes religiously downcast, may be thinking only of her ribbons. Let me see her eye light up as she speaks of Christ. Yonder manly boy may be so regular an attendant at church because of godly parents, or even because of the pretty girl. Let me hear his strong young voice lifted in prayer, and I can soon tell you.

"He has gone back on his — act." Did you ever hear that? No. "She has gone back on her — face." Did you ever hear that? No. Why is it that we always say, "He has gone back on his — word," if there is not something about words that is more trustworthy than other modes of expression? Do you wonder that they are expected of Christians?

Too Selfish to Speak.

The third reason why so much stress is laid upon vocal Christianity is because a lack of it implies selfishness. "I cannot express myself" means often, "I am too selfish to express myself." We hesitate to speak of Christ's glory, because we fear that we can get no glory by our speech. We do not lose ourselves and all thought of ourselves in thought of our theme.

O, of course, selfishness can produce clamor. It can make of us noisy word-mongers, eager to cry out anything that will draw men's attention to us. But from your personal experience tell me: has not selfishness been at the bottom of your ignoble silence more often than of your ignoble speech?

The Contagion of Dumbness.

In the fourth place, we object to silent Christians because failure in one mode of expression hinders success in all; vigor in one mode of expression promotes success in all. When your chat with your friend is the gayest, are not your smiles the warmest? When your words have been most fervently spoken for the dear Master, is not your life most fervently lived for him?

Our only safety, friends, is to be ready for obedience to the Holy Spirit in all modes of expression, so that whether he bid us walk or talk, laugh or weep, work or rest, it is all one blessedness to us. We dare not risk sloth in the tongue, lest it spread to the fingers and feet, the brain and the heart.

A Lofty Faculty.

The fifth reason is because we all feel that expression is one of the very best things in man, and we feel that religion should put man at his best. Milton said, in effect, "If you would write an epic, your life must be an epic"; but I would add that you cannot live an epic without in some way expressing an epic that all may read or hear.

So thought Gray when he wrote about "a mute, inglorious Milton." A mute Milton would indeed be inglorious, a living treason to his Creator. Equally treasonable would be a mute, inglorious Christian.

Words Fix Ideas.

In the sixth place, nothing so assures us of spiritual things and fixes them for us, as giving them outward embodiment. A man learns the full charms of his beloved one by recounting them to his mother. He discovers the dear beauty of his mother's life in telling his friend about her. He perceives most clearly God's love for him when he tries to tell it to others. He is weak in duty-doing until he has acknowledged that duty before his fellows. The truth he knows seems only half true until he knows that somebody else knows it. He knows that prayer is answered, but how much more he knows it when he hears you say that prayer is answered!

You are a stronger Christian than I am, if your belief does not go stumbling without the arm of another's belief; and you are a stronger Christian than I am, if you dare feel a thing to be right and true and required of you without instantly binding your belief to life by spoken profession of it.

The Magnifying Power of Speech.

And not only does expression fix what we have, but, in the seventh place, it adds to what we have. Christ's parable-servant simply *expressed* his pound, and it grew to ten cities. The foolish servant simply said that he could not express his pound, and from him was taken away what he had. Honest words spring up as life — a larger life than the words call for. And this larger life drops down words — still greater words than the life calls for. And so the blessed circles widen.

I want to say very earnestly that we are indeed clumsy and thriftless about our living if we neglect this powerful aid to growth. Let it not trouble us if our life lags behind our words, so long as it is struggling to catch up with them. Let it not trouble us, either, if our words lag behind our life, so long as they are struggling to catch up with it. A growing soul grows by the very fact of this interchange of goals, expression now leaping ahead of reality, reality now leaping ahead of expression, neither content ignobly with its present place. And so expression is expected of a growing Christian.

Missionary Tongues.

The eighth point and the last is this: speech is missionary power. With the mouth confession is made not only to our own salvation, but to the saving of others. The mere physical effort means something, the mere contraction of such muscles and vibration of so many tons of air, were that all there is of it. But when I am made to feel, as in all sincere speech I am made to feel, that over the flying bridge of your words your own true soul is speeding to me, it moves me as nothing else can.

This flutter of thin air against a stretched membrane backed by a chain of bones and a thimbleful of liquid, — what a trivial affair it is to make such bother over; and yet it is by just this foolishness of preaching, of your trembling words and mine, that the kingdom of God is to come. It is not ours to tell why there is power in it. It is ours to recognize the fact that the Father has placed great power there, and humbly to take up the tool he hands us.

And now I have given my eight reasons for setting such high value on expression in religious life. Let me repeat them. Ready speech is common in all other earnest work, and so should not be absent from Christianity. Speech furnishes a quite unmistakable mode of expression of our faith. A lack of it implies that self is too much with us, that we are not fully God's and man's. A failure here means, by the sad contagion of weakness, comparative failure in all other modes of expression. Speech is one of the loftiest of human powers, and should attend the loftiest human experience. Words fix for us the spiritual truth we feel. Words enlarge life, to be in turn enlarged by life. Speech is God's chosen missionary power. There are enough good reasons, surely, to stir any of us Christians from unchristian silence.

And now for the last topic of this chapter. If the activity of the tongue is so valuable, how may we get it? I have precisely ten rules, which I wish briefly to give you.

The Longing for Power.

First rule for obtaining freedom of expression: want it. I am sometimes tempted to be very impolite when I hear people say, "How I wish I could speak or pray in prayer meeting!"

"Wish!" I want to exclaim. "Why, you have n't even the desire of a wish! By their fruits ye shall know them, — wishes, as well as everything else. Do men gather dumbness from longing, or sluggishness from desire? One hearty wish would at least bud into one timid little word."

Let us not cheat ourselves. A desire for the ability of expression means vastly more than envy of some one who has it, or uneasy sense that we are not doing our duty. It means that earnest asking for a thing with the prayer of our whole being, which Christ said always finds what it seeks. We can never get power of expression until we thus want it.

Nothing for Nothing.

Second rule: work for it. Zeal is the mother of expression, but observation is its father. Study those that have this power, to imitate, not their manner, but their method of obtaining their manner. Ask them how they overcame your difficulties. Read widely, especially in the best expressed of all books, the Bible. Think seriously, not scorning the thoughts God gives you. Write constantly; nothing better drills the tongue than the pen. Talk in private on the themes which will be your public topics.

Ask advice, read, think, write, converse; in all these ways you must work, if you truly want the power of expression.

The Week Before.

Third rule: make preparation. Not merely the general preparation I have outlined, but special preparation for each occasion. "Why," some one objects, "did n't Christ say, 'It shall be given you in that same hour what you shall speak'?" Yes, but whom was Christ then addressing? His chosen disciples, men who had left all to follow him, men whose every moment was engaged in the most active and effective preparation for public speech.

And that is the only kind of special preparation I would advise you to make. Fill yourselves full of the subject. They spent their lives in that task; do you spend half an hour daily? If you wish to take part in the next prayer meeting, during that daily half hour for a week think over the subject; read about it, in the Bible especially; write on it; pray over it. At the end of the week you will have too much to say.

Have you ever seen a flower open? A few minutes ago it was hidden modestly in its green wrappings, and now it startles us by its splendid beauty

Surely God gave it in that hour what it should speak. Surely there was no rehearsing of that opening. No; but what a life of preparation, from the flower to the bud, back to the stem, the two little tentative leaves, the seed, the rootlets, the soil, the sun, the rain, the geologic æons! A Christian should indeed speak *ex tempore*, out of time, out of such a whole lifetime of preparation.

Step by Step.

Fourth rule: be content with small beginnings. That is, be content with that wherewith God is contented; only, he has made you so near the angels that it is impossible for you to begin anything with as small beginnings as he himself has had to make in his work of creation.

The parable of parables for the young Christian is that of the mustard seed. He must be content to sow the shortest of all prayers, the briefest of all sentences, the most stammering and awkward expressions, and if he have faith as a grain of mustard seed, his words will take root in good and honest hearts, and when they are grown they will be strong trees.

A Noble Ambition.

But I must immediately set off against this rule my fifth: never be content with less than the best possible at the time. That will prevent your being content with small continuations of small beginnings.

Best runs, while Second-best stands still. We have so few strong Christians, because we have so few weak Christians that are willing to be as strong as they can be. Being perfect as our Father in heaven is perfect, — why, that means nothing more than doing our best every time. Take care of your best, and growth will take care of itself.

A Cure for Stage Fright.

Sixth rule: come to understand your physical insignificance and your spiritual significance. When I find myself in danger of stage fright, weak knees, shaky hands, chattering teeth, ideas chaotic, I start my mind off on a trip around this great earth, stretching so far in its vast, rounded bulk that all the swarming millions of men could be packed into a little, unnoticed corner of its surface. My nerves begin to steady a little.

Then I set off on a voyage to the sun. I try to fancy myself walking swiftly day and night for long thousands of years before I reach it, and as I gaze back over the unimagined distance, the whole world with its speck of humanity looks too small to be afraid of.

Once more I start, this time not on foot or with the wings of the wind, but with the wings of light, — light which can girdle this great earth more than seven times while your watch ticks once. At that speed I fly for three years until I reach the nearest star, and then look back.

I have gone far enough. All my fear of my fellows is lost in a sense of their insignificance and my own. Now, I would as soon be afraid to address a thousand ants, as a thousand men. And as I hasten back from my fancied journey, I need now to spur myself to expression by reminding myself how expression is worth while; for indeed all things human are in danger of seeming too trivial, swallowed up in the thought of the greatness of God. I must remember how we little men are made in the image of the mighty Father, how sadly we have stained that noble image, how the Father himself came down into our pettiness, and dignified it forever. My bashfulness is all gone now, and awe and zeal have taken its place.

Put Self Behind You.

This, too, has led me to my seventh rule for gaining expression, which is: become unselfish. Do not stop with dwarfing self by thoughts of your physical insignificance, or with exalting self by thought of your spiritual significance, but go on to the forgetting of self's littleness or greatness in remembrance of your brother's need.

Do you know that there is nothing which so hinders expression as the comparative degree? Am I speaking worse, or better, than some one else? Am I doing more or less excellently than the occasion demands? The comparative degree stamps with comparative failure everything that it touches. No person ever expressed himself well while he was thinking about expressing himself well, or about another's expressing himself well.

I do not know what professors of elocution and oratory would say, but I think that all helpful expression is conditioned on self-forgetfulness.

Expect! Expect!

My eighth rule is: speak in the attitude of expectation. Expect to win people's attention, and you will win it. Expect to touch men's hearts, and you will move them. Expect to stir them to action; your words will reap a harvest in no other way.

Too much of our talk is in what a blundering scholar of mine, stumbling pardonably among Greek roots, once called the past-present tense. Much more of our talk should be in the future-present tense, should look with present, vivid confidence to definite outcomes. Expression of what has been is easy and natural for the old, and the young sometimes think it their duty to imitate them. But the natural attitude for youthful expression is the forward-looking one, which anticipates.

Act Out Your Speech.

Ninth rule: remember that, as I have hinted, the best seed of a word is a deed, just as the best seed of a deed is a word. If you want to learn to talk eloquently on the advantages of church membership, try to get some one to join the church. If you want to speak beautifully on the uses of sorrow, try to comfort some one who is mourning. If you want to become strong in combating scepticism and in expressing faith, try to strengthen some particular doubting Thomas. To every form and subject of expression there are appropriate deeds, which will create it wise and beautiful.

Our Example and Power.

Tenth rule, and last: let Christ be your example of expression, and the Holy Spirit your power. No man ever spoke as Christ did, but we may reflect his image, growing from glory to glory in our words as well as in our faces and our lives.

I think I see in those that are the closest students of the blessed Book, a constant approach to Christ's directness and divine simplicity, to his skill of dramatic portrayal, and the power of his language over the heart. With Christ as our example, we shall speak, not to please men, not with cunning craftiness, but as the Father directs who dwells within us. Let me tell you a parable.

In a Figure.

A marble block lay roughly hewn out from the quarry. The Poet passed by and said, "Statue, goddess, form of beauty hidden in this marble, — I can see your lovely curves, I can see your glorious smile, though no one else perceives you."

And as he passed, the block was filled with delight and satisfaction. "I have no need, then," it thought, "of the torture of hammer and chisel. Inner being is enough, without outward seeming."

But the next day the Moralist came near, and seeing the marble block he said, "Alas, here is this marble, pure for a statue of Mary, strong for a statue of Paul, yet all ugly and misshapen! How futile is inner reality without outward form!"

Then, as he went on his way, the block fell into great unrest. "Come, rain and sun," it cried, "and wear away the imprisoning crust. Come, wind, and dash it off, and show the world my hidden beauty!"

Then the sun and rain came, and weathered the marble in great, unsightly holes. Then the wind came and tossed it about, cleaving off great slabs here and there. The block was uglier than before, so that the quarrymen passed it now with a shrug of their shoulders.

But one day the Artist visited the quarry, seeking a block for his statue. "Take me, O take me," moaned our battered marble. "Do with me what you will; torture me with hammer and graver; for you alone can free my beauty from its ugly shell."

And the artist did choose it, and after many sorrows and long toil it shone one of the world's most marvelous statues.

Would that thus we too, crude human souls seeking the expression of the divine within us, learning of a surety that outer seeming must attend inner being, may learn also to disavow the elements of this world, and trust for the expression of ourselves to the great Artist alone.

O Lord, open thou our lips, and our mouths shall show forth thy praise.

CHAPTER II.

THE GENERAL WORK OF THE COMMITTEE.

Organize Your Committees. — It is not enough for the prayer-meeting committee to have a chairman; it is also well for it to appoint a vice-chairman, to assist the chairman, and take charge of the committee if the chairman is necessarily absent. The committee should also have a secretary, who should keep the minutes of the committee meetings, and, possibly, prepare the report, though the report should always be submitted to the other members of the committee for suggestions, and the chairman of the committee may probably consider it his own privilege to write it. The committee meeting should be carried on after the manner of the business meeting of the society.

A Committeeman to a Meeting. — Though of course the chairman of the prayer-meeting committee has general charge of all the prayer meetings, yet it is productive of good results to assign each meeting to the special oversight of one of the committee. The committeeman in charge for the night should help the leader by talking over the topic with him, lending him a Christian Endeavor paper and other helps, assisting him to find suitable hymns, and suggesting methods of leading. If for any reason the leader fails to appear, the prayer-meeting helper for that night should be prepared to lead, and should take the chair immediately.

The Verse-Reader's Class. — That is indeed a happy society that contains no verse-reader's class, or no class of those that I must consider quite as bad, if not worse, — the members that always take part in the meeting by reading brief quotations from well-known writers, making no comment upon them whatever, nor saying in any way that the quotations represent their personal experiences, or are presented as their testimonies.

One way to break up this habit of reading Bible verses or quotations from secular writers, and taking part in no other way, is to talk frankly to the members about the weakness of the practice. You must recognize the fact that often, very often indeed, there is no better way to take part than by repeating Bible verses; but this is not true when those who take part in that way do it on account of sloth, or baseless timidity, or carelessness.

When an Endeavorer repeats a Bible verse because of his love for that passage, because he is filled with gratitude for the comfort and strength it has brought into his life, because he wants others to share with him in this joy, and *says* something of all this, though only in a trembling sentence, — that is one thing; but when an Endeavorer repeats a Bible verse, or reads it from a hastily written slip of paper, hurrying over the words, and mumbling them so that they can scarcely be distinguished, his whole thought evidently to fulfill the letter of the pledge without caring for the spirit of it, — that is quite another thing. Often a frank talk along these lines, especially if it come from one of your most earnest members, or from the pastor, and if it be followed by a straightforward call for promises to forsake the habit, and add at least a brief comment to the verse that is quoted, will produce the very best of results, and win nearly the whole of the society from the verse-reader's class.

The first step will usually be to get the members to commit to memory the verses they make their testimony. Let this become the rule in your society. Appoint one of the prayer-meeting committee to observe the infractions of this rule, and to report the number of them at each society meeting, praising the society for whatever progress they may make in this line. Next get these verse-readers (or verse-repeaters, as they will become) to add just one sentence to the verse; such as, "I have come during the past week to see helpfulness in this verse"; or, "These words of Christ have become very precious to me"; or, "I want to take for my testimony this sentence from Paul."

The use of sentence prayers, and the frequent urging of all the members to take part in these chain prayers, will do much to draw Endeavorers from the verse-reading class. Personal work is needed here. Often you can get three or four of the timid members to promise to take part in sentence prayers, if all the others will do so. Sometimes the members of the prayer-meeting committee may pair themselves off with the timid members, each asking one of them to add one sentence to the prayer the committee member himself will offer when a chain prayer is called for.

It will be hard to win the Endeavorers from the verse-readers' class unless the better workers in the society themselves occasionally take part by merely repeating Bible verses, adding to them a very brief testimony. This will show the beginners in the work how to do it. Sometimes, too, it is a wise step to have a meeting that may be called a " Bible verse meeting," during which all will participate merely by repeating Bible verses bearing on the topic, adding sentence commentaries, or commentaries rigidly confined to two or three sentences. In the same way, quotation meetings may be held, the members being permitted to take part only by repeating from memory quotations from standard Christian writers regarding the topic of the evening, adding in each case a sentence or two of their own.

How to Obtain Promptness. — I have summarized in the following sentences some of the reasons for tardiness in attendance on Christian Endeavor meetings. If your society lacks promptness, it might be a good plan to have these reasons printed on a little dodger which could be distributed among the members : —

WHY YOU WERE LATE.

Because you did not plan to be early.

Because you did not notice other Endeavorers going to the meeting.

Because you do not own a consecrated watch.

Because you care more for your own ease than God's cause.

Because others are late and you are willing to train with them.

Because you have never thought about it.

Because the nice adjustment of your clothes is more on your mind than the success of the meeting.

Because you put off preparation till the last minute.

Because tardiness has become a habit with you.

Because you do not realize the power of example.

Because promptness is not expressly mentioned in the pledge, and you are a letter-Christian, not a spirit-Christian.

Because you have forgotten how you felt when you were leader, and your opening exercises were spoiled by late-comers.

Because you are a passive member, and not an active one.

> "Take my feet, and let them be
> Consecrated, Lord, to thee."

One of the best ways of curing this lack of promptness is to begin the meeting always on time. Let the prayer-meeting committee begin it themselves, if no leader is present, and even though a very few of the members are there. It is not best always to open with the singing of five or six hymns. These introductory song services are very pleasant, but if the society is inclined to dilatoriness, the opening song service will encourage it. The members do not feel that they are late if they arrive while it is in progress. Sometimes hold no song service at the opening, but begin with a service of prayer, or let the leader at once give his introduction.

One cure for this habit of procrastination is for the ushers to permit the first comers to take the back seats, thus forcing the late arrivals to march to the front. This disturbs the meeting, but may be made a gain in the end.

One society found it very effective to hang out in the front of the room, as soon as the exercises began, a large placard with the announcement, in bold type: "YOU ARE LATE!"

It is a good plan for the prayer-meeting committee to make a record, on consecutive Sundays, of the number that are late. Such a report, made at each meeting with suitable comments, is likely to bring about a gain in promptness.

In extreme cases, a report might be made to each member at the end of a month, stating how many times that member had been present on time, and how many times he had been late.

It needs to be said, also, that a prompt closing is as necessary as a prompt arrival. Indeed, a business-like, brisk way of conducting the meeting throughout will soon instill business-like habits in the members.

To Get Brevity. — There are those who hold that nothing worth saying can be said in a speech that is shorter than five or ten minutes. I suppose those who accept this dictum would sneer at a local union I once heard of which held a testimony service lasting about thirty minutes, in which, by actual count, one hundred and twenty-eight took part. I have no doubt that each one of those one hundred and twenty-eight said something that was worth saying and worth hearing. Critics call this a kind of "sacred game," but they might well be asked how long it took the publican to say, "God, be merciful to me, a sinner!"

No point in the new-fashioned prayer meeting which the Christian Endeavor movement is likely to establish is to be counted more valuable and important than the large number of persons that participate in each meeting, this large number being made possible by the conciseness of those who take part. In the pointed, straightforward testimonies common in our Christian Endeavor meetings quite as much is said as would, under other circumstances, be extended to occupy ten or fifteen minutes; and those sharp arrows go straight home to the consciences and lives of the hearers.

Occasionally, however, in all societies, the long-winded speaker crops out, and it is frequently necessary to insist upon brevity in the meeting. Let the president or the pastor speak plainly, take the number of members in the society, and the number of minutes in the time of meeting, and by simple division show each member how much time he can fairly claim, unless he considers that his thought is far more valuable than the thought of the others around him, — so valuable that he feels warranted in expressing it at length, though by so doing he makes it impossible for five or six others to speak at all.

Remind the members that other meetings are coming; that it is not necessary to say in one meeting all one feels or thinks or has experienced. Speak boldly to individual offenders in this regard; boldly, but lovingly, and in the spirit of Christ.

At the executive committee meeting discuss the matter, and instill a sentiment opposed to long-windedness. Get the better workers, those whose speech is most fluent, to set an example of brevity. Publicly commend the testimonies that are most brief and pointed, by repeating what they say, with a word of hearty approval. And, especially, show the members that brevity can be obtained only by careful preparation. The less one has thought about the subject, the more likely he is to talk at great length upon it.

The Preparatory Meeting.— It would be impossible for a prayer-meeting committee to devise a better method of deepening the spiritual interest in the meeting than that which has come, I am glad to say, into quite common usage,— the holding of a ten-minute prayer service preceding the Christian Endeavor meeting. This service is held by the prayer-meeting committee and the leader of the evening. Occasionally there may be added a few visitors especially invited for definite reasons.

During these few minutes of earnest petition for God's presence and power, the prayer-meeting committee will do its most efficient work.

A Preparation Class. — The preparation class is for the use of members that find it exceedingly difficult to take part in the Christian Endeavor prayer-meeting, either because of timidity, or because they do not know how to find thoughts upon the topic. This class should be led by one who is wise enough not to do the thinking of the members, but to teach them to think for themselves; to teach them how, by meditation and Bible-study, to discover God's truth.

In this preparatory meeting few will be gathered, and therefore those few will be less timid in expressing their thoughts. The topic of the evening will be discussed informally and will be prayed over, and the members that take part in this preparatory service will go into the larger meeting ready to contribute some original thought that will be helpful. If such a preparatory class were held no oftener than once a month, it would be of great advantage.

Workers' Training Classes. — The prayer-meeting committee might organize a training class for drill in methods of prayer-meeting work. The spirit of such a class should be one of great seriousness, and much prayer should be offered over the labors of the meeting. A wise and experienced worker should conduct the class, and all the prayer-meeting leaders, appointed beforehand for a number of months, should be gathered together for study and consultation.

Methods of leading as well as methods of participation will be discussed. Different kinds of prayer meetings and their fitness in connection with the different topics of the coming weeks, different ways of obtaining thoughts upon the subject, the use of quotations, the use of the Bible to illustrate the topic, the telling of experience, personal testimony, the use of the hymn-book, how to open the meeting, how to close the meeting, — these are samples of the topics such a training class might study.

A Prayer-meeting Scrap-book. — The most serviceable scrap-book for the use of the prayer-meeting committee will consist of a series of envelopes of uniform size, labeled appropriately to the clippings they are to contain. One should hold comments on the topic taken from Christian Endeavor and denominational papers. These will be especially valuable in following years, as similar topics come up. Others should contain methods of work, one envelope holding practical hints for leaders; another, suggestions regarding singing; another, points on the use of the Bible in Christian Endeavor meetings, etc.

Quotations from standard writers, poems suitable for use in prayer meetings, and the like, should also be divided among envelopes appropriately labeled. One, for instance, will contain the quotations on heaven, another those on truth, others those on peace, happiness, praise, promise, faith, etc. These envelopes should be kept in a box just fitted to them, and should be arranged in alphabetical order.

A Prayer-meeting Note-book. — The prayer-meeting committee should keep themselves, and should urge all the members to keep, prayer-meeting notebooks. It would be money well expended if the society were to present to each member some such book. In the books should be spaces for each Sunday in the year. At the head of each space should be written the topic for one Sunday.

In these books the Endeavorers will write whatever thoughts on the topics of coming weeks may come to them while they are about their business or their play, quotations from helpful poems, and illustrations taken from their reading or observation. If each Endeavorer keeps in mind the topics for seven or eight weeks to come, not only will he have no lack of something to say at every meeting, but the meetings themselves will be greatly deepened and enriched.

A Word of Praise. Praise is an important part of the duty of a member of the prayer-meeting committee. If an Endeavorer's words please you, if his prayer inspires you, if his singing uplifts you, say so. This will not be flattery, which ruins, but appreciation, which blesses him that gives and him that takes. Especially is it your duty thus to help the weaker members whenever you conscientiously can, and with none should you take greater heed to perform this duty than with the inexperienced leader, who is certain to think his first meeting a complete failure.

Helps for the Timid Members. — Many Endeavorers that are too bashful to take part in the meeting beyond reading a verse from the Bible, would be led to further endeavors by a definite request from the prayer-meeting committee. Such a request might be printed, couched in this language:

At the next Christian Endeavor prayer meeting, will you not rise and pray when opportunity is given? Three sentences will be enough. If you wish you may use the following subject: ....
Yours for the Master,
PRAYER-MEETING COMMITTEE.

Instead of asking the member to rise and pray, a request may be made that he take part in the sentence prayers. The following similar blank is useful for the same purpose:

> "Heaven is not reached by a single bound,
> But we build the ladder by which we rise
> From the lowly earth to the vaulted skies,
> And we mount to its summit round by round."

Will you not write a few sentences on the subject to read at the next meeting? Fifty words will be enough.
Yours in the work,
PRAYER-MEETING COMMITTEE.

A Young Women's Division. — If the young women of your society are backward about taking part in the meetings, it will be helpful to organize for a time a young women's division, which will meet just before the whole society, or at some time during the previous week. No one should be permitted to enter the young women's division that is already a skillful prayer-meeting worker.

The topic should be the one that is to be taken up at the coming meeting, and all that take part in the young women's division should consider this an extra service, in no way freeing them from the pledged duties to the regular society. Many of the older women of the church may be glad to join this division of the Endeavor society, to gain strength in it for the work of the mid-week prayer meeting of the church.

Cottage Prayer Meetings. — For many a prayer-meeting committee the work of carrying on their own prayer meetings is so easy that they are in need of outside work to do, and no committee could do a better work for its own society, whether the society is strong or weak, than by holding cottage prayer meetings in the homes of the sick of the congregation, as well as in the homes of those throughout the town that for one reason or another do not go to church, but are willing to receive such a service. These meetings are especially grateful to the aged.

The cottage prayer meeting, of course, will not require the attendance of the entire society, but the Endeavorers should be divided into bands, these bands agreeing to conduct the cottage services in their turn for a certain length of time, or possibly to take up throughout the year this work in some section of the town. Cottage prayer meetings are largely occupied with singing, and there should be much prayer, reading of the Scriptures, and helpful, comforting, and strengthening comments thereon, both prose and poetry. There should also be testifying, but this is a rare gift, and no one should hesitate to join the bands for holding cottage prayer meetings because he or she cannot testify eloquently. Often a beautiful poem sympathetically read, or a clear voice in the singing, will do as much for the meeting as some more formal testimony.

From these cottage prayer meetings important mission work is likely to grow. This work is taken up far more extensively by Christian Endeavorers in foreign lands than in our own, I am sorry to say.

Christian Endeavor Oratory. — For no ambitious reason, but solely for the cause of Christ, every Christian should earnestly seek the power of effective public speech. The prayer-meeting committee will score a good point if. on every suitable occasion they suggest to the Endeavorers what a field for the cultivation of Christian oratory is furnished by the Christian Endeavor prayer meeting. At the same time it must be made plain what oratory is, — that true eloquence consists in sincerity and straightforwardness, in having something to say that is worth saying, and in saying it in the fear of God. Upon this point the eminent Baptist minister, Russell H. Conwell, has the following to say:

The art of extemporaneous speech had been almost lost in this country up to the time when the Christian Endeavor movement began its great work. It was a very current idea in public opinion at that time that the uses of oratory were largely past. To be able to make an effective speech was considered somewhat old-fashioned, and was regarded as an accomplishment which must soon become a thing wholly of the past.

But the Christian Endeavor pledge, which required that every member should take some part in each meeting, has developed abilities for extemporaneous speaking which must have greatly astonished the pastors and churches where these organizations have prospered.

Timid boys and more sensitive girls have begun with trembling, and expressed themselves in broken sentences, or by a misquotation, at the beginning of their Christian Endeavor experiences, who now speak with fluency and beauty, putting their ideas in such concise and lucid form as to convince, attract, and entertain in the most delightful and helpful manner possible.

Using Christian Endeavor Papers. — Some societies subscribe for a copy of a good Christian Endeavor paper, that is given to the chairman of the prayer-meeting committee for the time being. After the chairman has read it, he cuts out all of the many committee helps, and pastes them in scrap-books for the use of the different committees.

A Unique Committee. — At least one Christian Endeavor society makes up its prayer-meeting committee from the president, vice-president, secretary, treasurer, organist, and chorister of the society. The officers are presumably the most active workers in the society, and thus a strong prayer-meeting committee is assured. Each officer in turn is held responsible for the meetings of one month. He leads the first meeting of the month, while the last meeting, the consecration, is always led by one of the church officers.

While this plan is not to be recommended for all societies, by any means, it may meet the need of certain churches.

Personal Work. — It is very difficult, often, to get our societies to doing personal evangelistic work. The following blanks, if printed, or worked off on a manifolder, may be used effectively by any prayer-meeting committee for the purpose of arousing the Endeavorers to their duty toward the unsaved:

Please fill out this blank and put it in the question-box:

During the past year have you spoken to any concerning their salvation, that you might lead them to Christ?
....

If so, how many?..........................

If you have not, will you do so during the coming week?..........................

Yours for Christ and the Church,
THE PRAYER-MEETING COMMITTEE.

"I will make it a rule of my life to pray every day."
Will you not remember in your daily prayers the following persons:

....
....

Yours in Christian Endeavor,
PRAYER-MEETING COMMITTEE.

Absentee Blanks. — It is a great mistake for the members of the prayer-meeting committee to emphasize merely the absences from consecration meetings, and say nothing about the helpful practice of sending messages to other meetings from which the members are obliged to be absent. Copies of the following absentee blank may be worked off on a mimeograph or other duplicating machine, and a supply given to each member of the society:

Members' Absentee Blank.

LITCHFIELD, ILL.,................, 189.....
Y. P. S. C. E., CHRISTIAN CHURCH.
Dear Endeavorers: Desiring to contribute my part toward the success of the next prayer meeting, I ask you to accept the following : —

....
....
....
....

Hoping the meeting will be one of interest and profit, and praying that God will abundantly bless our efforts in his name,
   I remain yours in Christian Endeavor,

                    ....

═══════════════════════════════════════

☞ If obliged to be absent from *any regular meeting*, kindly fill out above blank and send or mail to chairman of lookout committee.

Left margin: Remember Our Pledge.

Right margin: "We are laborers together with God." 1 *Cor.* 3 : 9.

A "Combine." — I have heard of eight boys in a Christian Endeavor society that entered into a written compact to make remarks or lead in prayer in every meeting for six months. The result was admirable. Prayer-meeting committees that have difficulty in inducing some of their members to take the next step away from the verse-readers' class may find in this a valuable suggestion.

Put Out Your Sign. — The Christian Endeavor society may well have a prominent sign on the front of the church, announcing the time of its meeting. In addition, on prayer-meeting nights there should be hung outside of the church or the prayer-meeting room a transparency like the following:

 Prayer-Meeting Tonight.
WELCOME!

A Shelf. — In each society meeting room the prayer-meeting committee should have a shelf or some other convenient place where it may put the society's topic cards, so that new members may readily be supplied. The shelf will be found useful also for slips of paper containing references appropriate to the topic, or for the transmission of bits of information, as well as of calls for committee meetings.

Watchwords. — The prayer-meeting committee can give a little inspiration to the society by selecting a watchword for each month. This watchword may be placed on the blackboard in the front of the room where the meetings are held, so that the members are reminded of it at every meeting. It should be suggested that at the consecration meeting the members tell in what way, if any, this watchword has helped them in their daily living.

CHAPTER III.

THE COMMITTEE AND THE SOCIETY.

Work Together. — The prayer-meeting committee should always work in close relations with several other committees. The music committee should frequently be in consultation with it, as many of the plans for the prayer meeting require special music and wise selection of hymns. The flower committee should transfer to the society room, whenever possible, the floral decorations they have placed in the church for the church services. The good-literature committee might aid any meeting by the distribution of appropriate tracts.

The missionary committee should have entire charge of the meeting devoted to missions, but suggestions from the prayer-meeting committee would be cordially welcomed. Above all, the lookout committee should be in league with the prayer-meeting committee, so that the plan of the meeting may always be such as to have the best effect upon the associate members, and upon other young people whose needs the lookout committee is striving to meet.

Meet Together. — The deliberations of the prayer-meeting committee would often be enriched and vivified by the presence of these committees whose work is along closely associated lines, such, for instance, as the lookout committee, or, less often, the music, missionary, and temperance committees. Of course the chairmen of all the committees come together in the executive committee meeting, but it is well, also, to bring together once in a while all committeemen whose work is along similar lines.

Practical Discussions. — Occasional exercises in the nature of committee conferences may be a useful feature of our prayer meetings. These committee conferences may occupy possibly fifteen minutes, and they should come at the beginning of the prayer meeting, so that the deeper spiritual impress may be left for the close. They should be led by the president of the society, or by the pastor, or by the chairman of the committee whose work is under discussion. A two- or three-minute paper may introduce the discussion, and there may occasionally be a question-box, or an answer-box; but the greater part of the time should be occupied with voluntary participation.

Take these as samples of the topics that may be discussed in these open parliaments: "How may our socials be made more helpful?" "How can we obtain more prayers in our meetings?" "What is the best time and method for the daily Bible-reading?" "How do you find the pledge helpful in your week-day life?" "In what ways may the music of our society be improved?"

Led by Committees. — Once in a while appoint a committee to take entire charge of the prayer meeting. The different members of the committee will be assigned different lines of work. One may take charge of the singing, another of the Bible-reading, others will divide the topic of the evening among them, saying a few words each. A series of meetings thus led by committees sometimes serves to wake up a society, the different committees vieing with one another to produce good meetings. This plan of course would not be a good one for a permanent arrangement, but the temporary adoption of it would get a society very pleasantly out of its ruts.

A Pause Committee. — A very useful adjunct to the prayer-meeting committee is a pause committee, which may be under the supervision of the prayer-meeting committee. The members of the pause committee agree to fill the breach whenever there occurs in the prayer meeting one of those dreadful pauses that sometimes come in the meetings of the most active society.

Where the members are not numerous enough to furnish this additional committee, the ordinary committees of the society may be asked to take up in turn, month about, the work of the pause committee; or sometimes it is found best to appoint for each meeting three or four Endeavorers, numbering them, and asking them to fill the pauses in the order of their numbers; or the same course may be pursued, using only the members of the prayer-meeting committee. Most commonly a pause occurs at the start, at the close of the leader's remarks, when he makes the portentous statement, "The meeting is now open;" and the pause committee should be especially instructed to fill this gap.

A Call for Ideas. — Active workers in the Christian Endeavor societies are sometimes likely to undervalue the opinions and practical wisdom of the younger members and those less prominent in the society work. Such a symposium as the following letter calls for would undoubtedly bring in, however, many valuable ideas, and, if nothing else was accomplished, would at least set the members of the society to thinking about the society work.

Here is the letter, copies of which should be made on a manifolder and handed to each Endeavorer, and a response be written and returned to the prayer-meeting committee, whose chairman will present to the society the most helpful points in the responses.

Dear Friend: In order that the service which the Y. P. S. C. E. is trying to render to the pastor, members, and congregation of the First Church may be increased, will you please answer by letter the following questions? Any criticism or suggestions which you may choose to give about the work of the society will be gratefully received, and treated as confidential if so desired.

For the prayer-meeting committee,

C. H. BIRD.

1. In your judgment is the society doing its work as well as could be expected?

2. If not, shall we improve our present methods of work, or shall we change them?

3. What changes, if any, would you suggest?

4. How can we best help to get all the young people of the church, especially the young men, interested in the work of the church, and get them willingly to take an active part in the same?

5. How can we increase the work which the society is doing, and yet have all the members feel, not that the increase is a call to a new duty or a new burden, but that it means that they are to have a new joy given them by being sent about the Master's work?

Weekly Encouragements. — It is an admirable plan to devote a few minutes of every weekly meeting to the recitation of encouragements. If any of the committees have met with especial success during the past week, if they have developed any new methods of working, if any individual members have received special blessings, or if any Endeavorers have observed deeds of kindness and helpfulness in others — such bits of good cheer should be presented at this time for the good of all. A few minutes devoted to this exercise will be not only a great stimulus to optimism, but will become, as the members prepare for them, an education in the noble art of looking on the bright side of things.

A List of Visitors. — Lists of visitors should be kept carefully in every Christian Endeavor society. One of the results of keeping such a list will be frequent hints given to the lookout committee regarding young people that are getting interested in the society and may easily be persuaded to become members.

Such a list might well take the form of an autograph album, the visitors being requested to sign their names with their own hands, at the same time giving their addresses. Thus they will have one tangible proof of the interest of the Endeavorers, and besides, the album furnishes a means of breaking the ice and entering into conversation with the strangers. The service may be undertaken by the lookout or the social committee, but it falls not inappropriately also to the care of the prayer-meeting committee.

Opening Questions. — I have heard of a Presbyterian society in which it is the custom to open every meeting with a series of questions propounded by the president, and referring to the wider work of the society. These questions are:

1. Does any member of this society know of a brother or sister who is seriously ill or permanently disabled?
2. Does any member know of children that do not attend any Sunday school?
3. Does any Endeavorer know of a case of extreme poverty and destitution within reach of our church?
4. Can any Endeavorer give the name of a suitable young person who is not a member of any Christian Endeavor society, so that we may send him an invitation to join?

These questions may suggest to other societies one very helpful way of keeping before the members the special endeavors of the society.

Signed. — If your prayer-meeting committee is in

the habit of using printed slips to invite strangers to the meeting, to urge increased faithfulness to the pledge, or the like, be sure that these printed slips are *signed* by the members or the chairman of the committee. In this way a personality is given to the document that renders it doubly effective.

Letters to the Home Society. — The prayer-meeting committee should urge all members of the society that leave town for a temporary absence, to write at least one letter to be read in the society. The absent member should of course visit during his absence all Christian Endeavor societies he can, observe their methods, and describe them for the benefit of his home society. Such letters should especially be written during vacations, and the reading of them will do much to keep up the interest of the society meetings during this otherwise somewhat dull period.

A Letter Bag. — The absent members of our societies are not sufficiently cared for. It will be a pleasant attention to make up for them occasionally a letter bag, as it might be called. This is a collection of short notes and texts made by the Endeavorers and gathered by the prayer-meeting committee for sending to the absent members. It will be better to let the society know beforehand to whom its letter bags are to be sent, in order that the notes may have as much personal flavor as possible.

CHAPTER IV.

THE COMMITTEE AND THE CHURCH.

For the Church Prayer Meeting. — The prayer-meeting committee may do very much to add to the interest of the prayer meeting of the church. Of course all the Endeavorers have promised to attend this, but not so many as should, probably, are taking part in it. For the latter purpose the prayer-meeting committee may well divide the society into four or five divisions, and assign each division to some week of the month, sending to the members some such request as the following:

> ....
> Our pastor would like to have you present and take some part in the REGULAR PRAYER MEETING on Thursday evening,..................
> If unable to be there, please send something to be read, or an excuse to the pastor.
> THE C. E. PRAYER-MEETING COMMITTEE.
> *West Stockbridge, Mass.*

Gradual Graduation. — It will be the fault of the prayer-meeting committee, largely, if the thought and prospect of graduation are not kept before the society. Bear in mind that the society is a training school, and that its work must all be done with an eye to larger work in the church. Remember that graduation from an Endeavor society should be, as the word implies, *gradual*, and so especially seek to bring about the participation of the Endeavorers, more and more as they continue in the work, in the prayer meeting of the older church members.

At first the Endeavorers may be induced merely to read a brief passage from the Bible, then to repeat it from memory, then to add a sentence or two of their own, then to offer a brief prayer or a short testimony. Young people often fail to realize how helpful a few words from them will be in a meeting of older folks, — how this delights them and encourages them.

Some Statistics.— The prayer-meeting committee should watch the work of the Endeavorers in connection with the midweek prayer meeting of the church. This, when they sign the pledge, they promise to attend. It is well to get at the facts by taking a census, the committee counting the number of Endeavorers present for a series of midweek prayer meetings. To prevent discouragement, count also the number of church members present. It will usually be found that the Endeavorers are more faithful to prayer-meeting attendance than the older church members, as indeed, considering their youth, they should be.

However, all the Endeavorers, or practically all, should, in remembrance of their pledge, be present at the midweek meeting, and the prayer-meeting committee should hammer away at the point, both in public and private, until this result is accomplished.

At the Midweek Service. — It will greatly help the Christian Endeavor society if its interests are brought frequently before the entire body of the church gathered together at the midweek prayer meeting; and if the older Christians are not reminded of the Endeavor society at this weekly gathering, whose fault is it? I have heard of a society that regularly appoints some Endeavorer each week to attend the midweek service and offer special prayer for the Christian Endeavor society.

In Their Care. — In some churches one of the midweek prayer meetings of each month is placed in charge of the Endeavorers. They aid the pastor in selecting the topic, the leader is chosen by the Christian Endeavor prayer-meeting committee, and the Endeavorers are made to feel that, though the older people take part freely, upon the young people rests especially the burden of the meeting.

A Front Seat Brigade. — A certain Christian Endeavor society was deploring the vacant front seats in the midweek and Sunday evening meetings of the church, and solved the problem themselves in a way that is possible for every Christian Endeavor society. Some one had proposed Christian Endeavor ushers, to coax people to occupy those seats. "What! young folks telling their elders where they ought to sit?" exclaimed another, in abhorrence. "Let us fill those seats ourselves."

And so it was. The leader of the next prayer

meeting stated the difficulty in about twenty words. "Now," said he, abruptly, "we want all of you Endeavorers who will promise to fill the very front seats, middle block, beginning at the front and keeping on back as far as the eighth seat, at every church meeting, unless already filled, — we want you to rise."

The Endeavorers, without a word of argument or pleading, rose, to the number of thirty-four. That was all there was of it. No, not quite all; those front seats have been filled ever since.

After Meetings. — The common order is to hold the Christian Endeavor services before the regular evening church service of Sunday evening. In many churches, however, the conditions will favor making the Christian Endeavor meeting an after service, to which can be invited all those that have been especially moved or attracted by the pastor's talk, and wish to have an opportunity either of confessing Christ or of testifying to their own faith. These will be gladly welcomed by the Christian Endeavorers.

Many pastors feel the great advantage of this after service, and the Endeavorers would be glad to aid in carrying it on. Besides that, when the Christian Endeavor service is held after the evening meeting, the pastor is enabled to tell by the testimonies of his Endeavorers what portion of his sermon has been especially helpful to the young people, and this is no slight gain. Doubtless, however, for most localities it is preferable to place the Christian Endeavor meeting before the evening service.

Older People in the Meeting. — One hears very little nowadays of the objection formerly made to the Christian Endeavor Society, that it would establish a line of demarcation between the old and the young people of the church. It has been abundantly proved that it does no such thing. It is partly the work of the prayer-meeting committee to see that so untoward a result never occurs in your church. Show the older Christians that they are wanted in the young people's meetings. Occasionally have a notice to that effect given out in the church, that there may be no mistake about it, and invite them personally, especially those that are not likely to come without the invitation.

Once in a while, call upon them by name to speak and pray in the meeting. If they take part at too great length, get the president to remind them frankly that they must be brief, in order that the many members present may have opportunity to keep their pledge. Instruct the leaders to call upon some of the older people to say a few words on the topic, calling out different ones at each meeting.

It is an admirable plan to give special invitations to attend the meeting to those of the older church people that are especially interested in the week's topic. If, for example, the topic concerns the relation between the Sunday school and the Christian Endeavor society, especially invite the Sunday-school superintendent to be present, and to speak. If the Junior work is to be considered, ask the teacher of the primary department of the Sunday school to be there, and to add her wisdom. If it is patriotic, invite some old soldier, or some office-holder. If the topic is prayer, call in some prominent prayer-meeting worker from the older prayer meeting. Give frequent special invitations to the pastor and the church officers to take part on particular topics.

Pastor's Evening. — Some societies have the pleasant custom of giving one evening of each month into the hands of the pastor, who conducts the service as he pleases, of course giving an opportunity for all to take part as usual. Generally, however, the evening takes the turn of discussions of different phases of church work. One of the interesting features is a question-box, open to all the members, and conducted by the pastor.

A Church Officers' Meeting. — Get all the church officers and the pastor to attend this meeting, and let a representative from each department of the church work give a short talk to Endeavorers concerning his field of activity. Here is a suggested programme:

Three ways in which the Christian Endeavor society can help the pastor.

Three ways in which the Christian Endeavor society can help the deacons.

Three ways in which the Christian Endeavor society can help the trustees.

Three ways in which the Christian Endeavor society can help the Sunday-school superintendent.

How can the Christian Endeavor society help the committee on visitation?

How can the Christian Endeavor society help the ladies' missionary circle?

Can the Christian Endeavor society help the ladies' aid society? If so, how?

An Honorary Members' Meeting. — The entire charge of this meeting is to be placed in the hands of the honorary members, namely, the officers of the church, the Sunday-school superintendent, and such of the older members of the church as wish to maintain a connection with the society but cannot keep up active membership. One of these is to be the leader, and especial pains is to be taken to obtain a full attendance of this class of Endeavorers. The result of such a meeting would doubtless be to add greatly to the interest the honorary members take in the society and the society in the honorary members.

With the Pastor. — Divide the society into sections containing about eight persons each. To each section apportion some timid and some experienced members. To each of these divisions a week will be assigned.

Fifteen minutes before the opening of the prayer meeting for that week. the division will meet in the pastor's study with the pastor, the prayer-meeting committee, the president, and the leader for the evening, to kneel and pray for the meeting to follow. It is understood that they are to take part in the same order at the very opening of the following meeting.

CHAPTER V.

AT HOME.

Preparation for the Meeting. — The prayer-meeting committee should have an oversight of the preparation the members make for the prayer meetings. Let them occasionally speak in the meetings, urging more thoughtful and painstaking preparation. It is a good plan to buy a lot of cheap note-books, of convenient size for the vest pocket, and sell them to the Endeavorers at cost, that they may be used, in accordance with a suggestion before made in this book, as thought-books for the Christian Endeavor topics. Let each topic, and the Scripture reference for each week, be given a separate page, and urge the Endeavorers to look forward for six or seven weeks to come. If these advance topics are kept in mind, they will all be astonished to see how many appropriate hints they will glean from their newspapers and other reading, and how many thoughts will come to them as they go to their work.

Besides this, the committee may get the members to take thought for the meetings some time in advance, by themselves making mention of future meetings. It would be useful if one member of the prayer-meeting committee should take it as his especial work to look up books and articles that throw light on the next week's topic, and speak of these at each prayer meeting. Once in a while, call for prayer for the next prayer meeting, that an especial blessing may be vouchsafed to it.

Occasionally get the leader for the next week to speak, in the prayer meeting of the present week, regarding his plans for the next meeting, calling for whatever co-operation he desires. If, for instance, the topic is prayer, he might ask the members to speak, each of them, on some Bible prayer; or to come prepared to tell some occasion in their own experience, or the experience of others, on which prayer has been especially helpful; or he might ask for a committing to memory of brief poems regarding prayer; or he might ask the members to write out their heart experiences in the matter, for him to read.

The prayer-meeting committee should keep before the society a standing offer to help those that find it hard to prepare for the meeting, but the committee should themselves seek out those whose participation in the meeting shows that they are in need of such assistance, and should spend for these their chief energies.

It would be of service for some skilled worker with the Bible to take a quarter of an hour at the Christian Endeavor meeting to show the Endeavorers just how to use Bible index and concordance, in order to obtain light on the prayer-meeting topics. On occasion a capable Endeavorer might give a simple, practical lesson regarding the use of the hymn-book. Any hymn-book with a good topical index at the back, will furnish a large number of beautiful thoughts on any of the prayer-meeting topics.

On still another week, put forward a practical worker to illustrate the use of the questions on the topic given in THE GOLDEN RULE each week. These are for the purpose of stimulating thought, and suggesting themes for expansion in the meeting. This Endeavorer should take the questions for the next meeting, one after the other, read them, and show how, if the questions are followed up, each one of them will furnish the Endeavorer with an admirable little talk.

There are certain questions, moreover, that will always bring out the meaning of a prayer-meeting topic, and the prayer-meeting committee should teach the Endeavorers to ask these questions for themselves. For example: "What does this topic mean for me?" "How does it touch my common daily life?" "If I should put into my life the truth it suggests, how would it change things?" "What illustrations of this topic have I seen in life, or noticed in my reading?"

It will not be easy for the prayer-meeting committee to get the members to think for themselves, but that is the primal requisite for helpful participation in the prayer meeting; and the committee should stick to it until they have awakened every Endeavorer in the society, and put an end to all meaningless and perfunctory modes of participation.

Getting Something to Say. — I copy here a little article I once wrote, in the hope that it may show prayer-meeting committees how to deal with the Endeavorers that find it very hard to join actively in the meetings.

"How can I ever take part in the Christian Endeavor meeting?" This question is often heard. "I have no original ideas. I am not gifted in that way. I can read a verse of the Bible, and that is all I can do."

Well, if that were all you could do, dear Timid, that would be a great deal. A Bible verse, if said prayerfully and earnestly, is able to work the miracle of converting a soul. But it will be best *for you* if you add to this repetition of Scripture some word of your own, if you can. And I think that every one can, — every one, however bashful, and however he may think himself unfitted for the task.

If I were going to-morrow to attend a Christian Endeavor service, I should begin my preparation to-day — if, indeed, it were not begun several days ago. And this is the way I should go at it.

First, the subject is to be considered. Read it carefully. Think over it a little. Often this alone will tell you something you want to say.

Then read the Bible references and the daily readings for the week, if you have not already done so. There is no commentary like the Bible, nothing equal to it for quickening the mind. Probably by this time you have another thing you want to say.

Ask yourself how the topic affects you, what it has to do with your society and your church. Consider how your life and the lives of others would be changed if all should conform to the precepts of the lesson. Such thoughts will certainly give you something more to say, either of a personal or of a general character.

Look back into your past. Does it not teach you a lesson along this line? Have you no confession to make? Have you learned nothing on this point? Have your experience and observation shown you nothing that you could repeat for the good of your comrades?

Next, bethink yourself of your reading. Do you not recall some helpful poem in harmony with the subject of the meeting, a part of which you can repeat? Is there not some striking incident of which you have read that will point an appropriate moral? Has not some essayist expressed a thought that will give you the key-note of what you want to say?

Getting something to say? Why, dear Timid, just try faithfully and prayerfully all these sources and stimuli of thought, and, my word for it, your puzzle will then be, not to find something to say, but to choose among the many things you want to say the one thing that, on the whole, will be most helpful to your comrades in Christian Endeavor.

Speaking in Meeting. — Many who have most excellent things to say in our Christian Endeavor meetings fail of the highest usefulness because they do not say them in the best way. Almost invariably the fault is in the manner of preparation. I wish to give a few hints, not to the experienced speaker, but to the beginner in this prayer-meeting work.

I will suppose that you have the thought you wish to present, that you are greatly in earnest regarding it, and want to put it in the most effective way before your fellow Christians. How will you go at it?

Write it out. Yes, *write it out!* What is written is fixed in the mind as it can be in no other way. If it does not please you in the first form, write it out again, and again, until the thought is expressed as neatly and forcibly as you can put it.

Then tear up what you have written. Yes, tear it up into the finest possible bits. Don't try to remember the words you have written. You are not going to speak a piece. You are going to speak a thought.

Try to give speech to your thought now, in the quiet of your own room. Fancy yourself addressing the society. Don't think how you are saying it,— just *say it*. Can you do this clearly and without hesitating? Then wait a few hours, and see if you can do it again. Say it as you go about your work, on the streets, as you dress in the morning, whenever you have a spare minute. You may say it every time a different way. When you go to say it before the society you may say it in a way different from any of these ways. What is the harm?

If possible, talk the matter over with some one who will sympathize with you. Nothing clarifies one's ideas better than conversation. The other Endeavorer, too, will want to talk over his thoughts with you.

When you come to the meeting, don't think about yourself. Don't think about your words. Don't think about the impression you are making. Don't be silly in any way. You are just one of God's little children, and those folks around you are just God's little children, every one of them. And you are telling them something that God has given you to say. You are not making a speech. You are not making an impression. Indeed, it is not you that is speaking, if you are speaking rightly, but it is God who is speaking through you. Why should you not speak boldly, and simply, and lovingly, and — for this is only a condensation of these three — eloquently, also?

A Prayer List. — It will prove a help to your society in their daily devotions, if you present to each of them a printed list, that may be prepared on a manifolder, containing the names of the active, the associate, and the absent members of the society. Each name is dated, and on every day all the members are to pray for the one whose name is on that day.

Pray Aloud in Private. — The prayer-meeting committee will do much to get the Endeavorers to take part by prayer in public meetings, if they can persuade them to make it a habit to pray aloud in their private devotions. This will seem strange and confusing at first, but in a while the practice will tend to concentration of thought. The petitions will become more earnest and extended, and, best of all, the Endeavorers will become able to pray aloud in public without any feeling of constraint.

Special Prayers.— The prayer-meeting committee may often introduce into the private devotions of the members of the society much directness and power by occasionally requesting special prayers during the coming week for certain particular objects. For instance, if the president or some committee of the society has undertaken any especially difficult work, let prayers be requested for their success. If any member of the society is in special trouble, ask for petitions in his behalf. If any special cause for thanksgiving arises, ask for prayers of praise. The results of such directions, though hidden, cannot easily be estimated.

Suggestions for Prayer. — The daily devotions of the Endeavorers will be likely to have power in proportion as they have definiteness. The following suggestions for themes for daily prayer may be printed by a manifolder and given to each, or a place may be found for them on the society topic cards.

SUGGESTIONS FOR DAILY PRAYER.

Believing that God will grant a special blessing in answer to united prayer for definite objects, the prayer-meeting committee requests you, as a member of our society, to remember in prayer, every week, the following objects on the days named:

SUNDAY. — Our church, our pastor; that by means of the services to-day, Christians may be strengthened and souls may be won to Christ.

MONDAY. — Our society of Christian Endeavor, its officers, the prayer meeting and its leader; that we may all remember that we are servants of Christ.

TUESDAY. — Our Sabbath school, its officers and teachers; that the teaching and the life may prove the truth of the gospel.

WEDNESDAY. — Onr church prayer meeting; that we may all see and do our duty in regard to it; that all Christians may bring forth much fruit through abiding in Christ.

THURSDAY. — The young people in our church who have not declared themselves on the Lord's side; that they may soon know and own Christ as their Redeemer and Lord.

FRIDAY. — The members of our church that are "shut in"; that Christ may be "all in all" to them. The children; that they may be kept "from the evil."

SATURDAY. — All who are working for Christ at home or in foreign lands. "Pray ye therefore the Lord of the harvest, that he will send forth laborers into his harvest."

"And all things, whatsoever ye shall ask in prayer, believing, ye shall receive."

CHAPTER VI.

THE LEADER.

Appointing Leaders. — Many prayer-meeting committees make the mistake of going around to the members whom they desire to have lead the prayer meetings, asking each one in turn if he will lead upon a certain night. The committee should find out at the beginning of its term of office how many members are willing to lead the meetings. They may be asked to lead without any further notice than an announcement before the society, or upon a topic card or a bulletin board, or by postal card. Most of the members of any society will give the prayer-meeting committee this permission, it being always understood, of course, that if for any reason they cannot lead the meeting at that time, they will give the committee ample notice. This arrangement will save the committee much time and worry, and will at the same time exemplify in the society the spirit of Christian Endeavor.

Of course the committee will not get this permission from all the members, and in appointing leaders they should seek also to enlist in the service the more backward and less willing Endeavorers. It is a temptation for the committee to summon to the leadership only the more active workers, but this would be a great mistake, since the Christian Endeavor Society is pre-eminently a training school. If anything, there should be a preponderance of unskilled, timid, inexperienced leaders.

Take especial pains to get the new members to lead, as soon as you think they are quite at home in the society work. There is no better way of introducing them to the society, and of thoroughly settling them in their fellowship.

When the Juniors are graduated into the older society, they should be given the leadership of meetings as soon as possible. Remember that they are accustomed to lead, and that it is particularly necessary for them to feel that they are not to be forced into the back seats.

If there are any members that object very seriously to leading, do not tease them; simply show them that you wish them to lead, and consider it their duty to do so, using few and earnest words. Accept their refusal in a cheerful spirit, but be sure to return to the charge a few weeks or months later, and keep their consciences active in the matter, until you have won them to make an attempt.

One of the best methods of helping those who are timid in this service is the plan of double leadership. Couple together the timid with the more experienced. The experienced worker will take the chief direction of the meeting and do the more difficult work, such as making introductory remarks and offering the opening prayer, but the reading of the Bible passage, the announcement of the hymns, and the like, should be put into the hands of the more timid of the pair. He may also read a few words of his own concerning the topic. Sometimes, if the society is large, there may even be more than two leaders, each of them speaking on one subdivision of the topic.

The prayer-meeting committee should always see the member who is to lead the next meeting a week beforehand, to make certain that he is in town, and has not forgotten his coming duty. It is at this time that the committee should propose to the leader whatever plans they may have for the conduct of that meeting.

Fit Leaders to Subjects. — In selecting the leaders, the prayer-meeting committee should bear in mind the subjects to which each is assigned and the characters of the various Endeavorers. It would be unwise, for example, to assign such a topic as "Sorrow and its Uses" to one whose life has been all sunshine, or such a theme as "The Duty of Happiness" to a sour and long-faced Endeavorer, — if such an anomaly is in existence. Be sure that your leaders, so far as possible, are fitted by character and experience to treat with force, or at least without striking inappropriateness, the topics to which they are assigned.

Associates for Leaders. — I should never invite an associate member to lead a Christian Endeavor prayer meeting. Our leaders should always have as their chief aim the winning of souls to Christ. **One that has not already come to the Master cannot well give an invitation to others.**

In Alphabetical Order. — Some societies that do not intend that any member shall fail of the joy of leading the prayer meeting, arrange their members' names alphabetically, and each leads when his letter is reached. The advantage of this is that there is less likely to be shirking, and every one, moreover, knows when his turn comes. The disadvantage — and it is a serious one — is that thus it is rendered impossible for the committee to select leaders especially fitted to the topics they are to discuss.

Leaders in Rotation. — After all, one of the very best ways of selecting leaders for the Christian Endeavor meetings is to take the list of the society and have it distinctly understood that each member will lead once during a certain number of months. It will be necessary to shift the list a little in order to get appropriate leaders for the different topics, or in order to accommodate the members that cannot well be present on certain dates.

But the essential thing is that the society shall establish a universal custom of leading. Where all are expected to lead, new members as well as the experienced, and timid as well as courageous, few will even attempt to shirk. Some societies think it a loss not to keep in the leader's chair the more experienced members. I am persuaded, on the contrary, that the more timid and stammering leaders have the best meetings, since all rally to their assistance, and the experienced members can do nearly as much for the success of the meeting in the audience as in front of it.

Alternate. — Some societies find it especially difficult to persuade the young ladies to lead the meetings. Others have a lack of young men. Many a society, therefore, will find it advantageous, at least for a part of the year, to insist upon young men and young women alternating in the leadership of the meetings. Those that otherwise might be quite reluctant to undertake the task will enter upon it under such circumstances.

A Leader's Help. — Some societies have adopted the plan of having the president sit on the platform with the leader of the prayer meeting. When a society contains even a few timid members — and what society does not? — this plan will be found very helpful in giving them courage and skill in conducting the meetings. Besides, it keeps the president prominently before the society and keeps his hands on the reins.

Leaders and Speakers. — Some English societies have the practice of appointing for each meeting not merely a leader, but what they call a speaker. The leader should be a good executive officer, able to conduct the meeting with despatch and vigor; but the speaker should be more glib in the use of his tongue. The leader may be one of the younger members, and the speaker one of the older ones. The leader will announce the hymns, set the meeting going, read the Scripture passages, and do other things of the sort, while the speaker will comment on the passages, and throw out suggestions for the general conduct of the meeting. Such Christian Endeavor "teams" should often be organized. They will give variety as well as effectiveness to our meetings.

Leader's Aids. — If all the members of your prayer-meeting committee are not able to give effective assistance to the leaders, they should be educated as soon as possible into this ability. Then you can carry out the admirable plan of appointing each member of the committee in turn to act as the aid for the leader for one evening. This aid will not only advise the leader as to the best way of carrying on the meeting, assisting him in planning for it, but will also be among the first to take part, to lead in any sentence prayers, start hymns impromptu, and in other ways seek to add interest to the evening.

Committee Leaders. — A society that happens to have twelve committees has the custom of appointing one of these committees to lead the first meeting of each month. The same plan may be tried, as suggested in a former chapter, with a smaller number of committees. A slight rivalry is developed, and the more timid members are educated into methods of leadership. Of course no one member of the committee has much to do, the work of leading being apportioned among the committeemen, to one or more the Scripture reading, to one the announcing of hymns, to one the prayers, to one or more the topic.

Ready to Lead. — It is well for the prayer-meeting committee to appoint one member each month who would be ready to lead the meeting in case of the unexpected absence of the appointed leader. Of course such absences will be rare, but it is well to be provided for them. Too often this duty of filling the place of a leader providentially detained falls on the chairman of the prayer-meeting committee or on the president.

A Notification. — A blank for notifying the member who is to lead the next prayer meeting will be found very useful. Such a blank is the following, that, with suitable changes, may be used by any society.

BOSTON, MASS., MAY 5, 1892.

Dear Brother : You have been appointed by the prayer-meeting committee to take charge of the Christian Endeavor prayer meeting on Tuesday next, May 10, with the subject of " Public Worship : a Privilege and a Duty," found in Ps. 84; Heb. 10: 25. We should be very much pleased to have you meet with our committee Sunday evening at 6.15, for the short prayer service. Trusting that you can comply with our request, I remain yours in the work for " Christ and his church," DAISY FLOWER,
        Chairman of prayer-meeting committee.

Some Hints. — If your society uses a blank for the notification of leaders, it is a good plan to place upon the back of it ten or twelve blank lines, headed : " Order of Exercises. Commence Promptly." Following the blank lines may be the words : " Collection"; "Closing Hymn "; "Benediction"; " Close Promptly," and also the following suggestions to leaders :

Call upon the president to make announcements just before you read the lesson and announce the topic.

Invite all strangers and any that are not members to take part.

Give the last five minutes of the meeting, before the collection, to the pastor of the church, if he is present.

Select hymns suitable to the topic.

Make your opening remarks brief.

Introduce sentence prayers.

A Reminder. — If your committee has difficulty in keeping before the leaders the thought of the meeting they have promised to lead so that they will prepare for it long enough beforehand, and notify the committee in case they are unable to lead, a good remedy is this: hang up on the wall of the meeting room a large placard on which are printed the topic, date, and leader for each meeting for some months ahead. No one in your society can then urge the excuse, "I did not know I was to lead."

Offer Your Services. — One of the most helpful things a member of the prayer-meeting committee can do is to go during the week to the leader of the next meeting and ask if he can be of any service in the meeting he is planning. Especially if the leader is an inexperienced and timid one, this inquiry will prove very encouraging. Even the most experienced leaders will be glad of such offers.

A Leaders' Conference. — One of the most helpful gatherings that could possibly be brought together in your society is a conference of the leaders of the prayer meetings for a quarter, or for a number of weeks to come. This conference would be presided over by the president, or by the chairman of the prayer-meeting committee, or by some skilled prayer-meeting worker. The topics for the coming weeks should be taken up and discussed one by one, no especial aim being made to furnish comment upon them, the point of the discussion being rather to contrive fresh ways of presenting the evening's truth, and new methods of bringing out the thoughts of members.

Some such book as the present would be peculiarly useful in leaders' conferences. The various methods herein suggested should have been studied beforehand by the leader of the conference, and he will present to the leaders of the coming meetings for their discussion and adoption whatever methods are most likely to be of service in connection with the topics of the quarter. The pastor should be present at this conference, and will greatly assist these deliberations. It would be well for the conference to be opened, if there is time, by a bright and brief paper on practical prayer-meeting methods.

Meet Early in the Week. — A word as to the time when prayer-meeting committees should meet with the leader for prayer and conference. If possible, this conference should be held sometime during the early part of the week, in order that the committee may suggest to the leader helpful ways of conducting the meeting. If it is held just before the meeting, an immediate stimulus is gained, but it is too late to form general plans.

Prayer-Meeting Programmes. — Of course every prayer-meeting leader should have a definite programme, containing a few novel features: possibly one would be enough for a meeting. Occasionally it is a good plan to print this programme on some duplicating machine, distributing the copies at the opening of the meeting. It is a good plan once in a while to print the programme in the town paper. This calls the attention of many to the work the society is doing, and may result in much good. Why should concerts have a monopoly of printed programmes?

Monthly Programmes. — It is a help to the prayer-meeting leader if he finds a programme already prepared for him, and in certain societies it may be found best for the prayer-meeting committee to lay down a definite programme for each month, these programmes being varied month by month. The programme for the month, in outline, should be printed in distinct letters, and posted before the society.

If there is any member of artistic skill, neatly drawn copies of the programme may be worked off on a mimeograph or hectograph. Possibly some amateur printer will be glad to print them. The programmes of consecutive months should be as different as possible.

Preparing to Lead. — Far too many leaders of our prayer meetings confine their preparation to getting something to say. That is the least of their business, their chief work being to get others to saying something; and it is toward this effort that the greater part of their preparation should tend.

The leader's chief aim in his remarks upon the topic should be not to say many things, or wise things, or primarily to say helpful things, but to say *suggestive* things, things that will set other brains to thinking and other spirits to feeling.

The leader should plainly suggest at the outset some ways in which the members may take part, provided they have no preference of their own, and his own participation should be rather in the way of setting them an example than to cover the ground.

The leader should come to the meeting having already assured himself that it will be a good one. He can do this only by advance work with the different members, asking one to speak upon this phase of the topic, another upon that; giving a poem to this backward member that he may read it, and a question to another that he may answer it; asking one to start a series of sentence prayers, and another to give an anecdote about some Christian life in harmony with the topic.

And after the leader in his preparation has decided what he will do and what he wants others to do, it remains for him to form a definite plan for the meeting, deciding precisely the order in which he wishes to introduce the different portions of his plan, and going over the meeting in his imagination many times, saying himself what he intends to say as if the audience were before him, and fancying the ways in which they will respond to his skillfully conceived designs. In all this, it need not be said, room must be left for change, addition, and compression, or for the entire abandonment of the plan, if the spirit of the meeting should make this necessary.

Vary the Opening. — The leader should bear in mind the way the meeting has been opened by the preceding leaders, and use a different mode. A fresh and vigorous opening will mean a meeting of vigor, while a formal, hackneyed manner of beginning will throw a damper on the meeting from the start.

Avoid such phrases as, "The meeting is now open." These do much to close the meeting instead of opening it. Vary the order of opening exercises, and draw the members of the society into them as far as possible, calling upon this Endeavorer to offer the opening prayer, upon another to read the Scripture, or, what is better possibly, ask the entire society to repeat passages of Scripture, in harmony with the subject of the evening, that occur spontaneously to their memory. Now sing several songs. On another occasion open the meeting without any singing at all.

It is a good plan sometimes for the leader to reserve what he has to say upon the subject until the conclusion of the meeting. If it has been said already, his saying it will merely add emphasis.

The leader's choice of opening should vary according to the results at which he aims. The opening may be made exceedingly informal, if formality is one of the society stumbling-blocks. It will make the Bible prominent, or prayer, or singing, or testimony, according as each of these will best contribute to the interests of the meeting.

The Opening Scripture. — It is not well for the leader of a prayer meeting invariably to read himself the passage of Scripture given for the evening. With this passage the members are all familiar, and in order to call fresh attention to it, it is a good plan to employ some novel method of reading. Sometimes the leader and an Endeavorer in the audience may read the passage, alternating verse about. Sometimes the passage may be divided, the leader reading the first three or four verses, then, by pre-arrangement, some Endeavorer taking it up and reading a few verses, and then another Endeavorer, or two more, completing the passage. Occasionally the leader may read from the authorized version, and another Endeavorer follow each verse with the same verse as rendered in the revised version. Two Endeavorers from the audience may read the verses responsively, and the exercise may be varied almost without limit.

Announce the Subject. — I have attended not a few prayer meetings whose leader took it for granted that every one in the room knew the subject of the meeting. It is never well thus to ignore strangers, even though every Endeavorer is familiar with the theme, which is not always the case. Besides, it clarifies the ideas even of those that have already thought on the subject to hear it distinctly stated, and told in several different ways, and this is the only businesslike course.

As your opening selections of song, the Bible reading, and the prayer, should all be in harmony with the topic of the evening, that topic should be announced before any of these exercises. At the outset of the leader's little talk on the topic, the theme of the evening should once more be stated. It is a good plan, as elsewhere suggested, to place the topic in distinct letters upon the blackboard, in plain view of all.

Select the Hymns Beforehand. — None but the most slovenly leader would think of undertaking the management of a Christian Endeavor prayer meeting without carefully studying the hymn-book for the purpose of finding the most appropriate songs. Bear in mind not merely the words of the songs, but the fitness of the music. Do not start with a slow and melancholy tune, however appropriate the words. Do not close, either, with a hymn whose music is trivial. It betokens a wise selection of hymns when the audience is sent away singing over again in the vestibule and on the street the song last used.

I do not believe in a too labored arrangement of the hymns, or in interpolated comments upon them, endeavoring to piece them together so as to make a musical discourse; and yet I believe that the hymns should all harmonize the one with the other, and if a progression of thought can be made apparent without forced interpretations, so much the better. At any rate, the leader should arrange the numbers of his hymns in order, and should never trust to haphazard selection of them.

Interrupting the Meeting. — It is a better fault for a leader to talk too little than too much. Of course an experienced leader, by interjecting some brief and pertinent commentary on what has just been said or read, can give point to a confused testimony, or make a timid, half-hearted speaker feel that he has indeed contributed to the evening in some noteworthy sense. On the other hand, there is scarcely any impertinence or hindrance to an effective meeting so great as a leader that is too prominent, that feels it incumbent upon him to make comments upon every Bible verse, to add a thought to all the testimonies, or even to interpret the meaning of the hymns. Only once or twice, at the most, in the progress of the meeting, should the leader interrupt at all, and then only when it is a clear case and he is sure of his ground.

Of course this does not apply to occasions when it is plainly the leader's duty to say a word, as when two or more start to speak or pray at once, causing an awkward pause, which the leader should promptly break by designating one person to speak, being sure on the conclusion of that testimony to call for the other. Or, if a meeting is near its close and some one inconsiderately calls for the first, second, and third verses of some hymn, it would be well for the leader to suggest that that hymn be made the closing one, and that the remaining time be given to prayer and testimony. Such interruptions as these do not, of course, come under the stricture of the preceding remarks.

To Fill a Pause. — One of the surest marks of a skillful leader is his ability to fill a pause in a prayer meeting. Sometimes, indeed, a good leader shows his wisdom by leaving the pause to take care of itself. That depends on the kind of pause, whether it is born of emptiness or of fullness.

The commonest mode of filling a pause is by singing. It is better, however, for the leader to start a prayer chain, if this exercise has not already been introduced. In each society, too, there will be members that are willing to be called upon to offer prayer. If a pause occurs, the leader may well say a few words reminding the members of the salient theme of the evening, and asking some Endeavorer to offer prayer along this line.

If the leader has made no remarks at the opening, he may utilize the pause in saying what he has come prepared to say. Again, he may start the current of thought by asking a few pertinent questions, or by reading a very brief quotation. Instead of calling for a song, it is almost always better, in case of a pause, to request the members to read in concert some appropriate hymn, whose words, thus vividly presented, will inspire fresh testimonies.

"Let Us Sing No. 24." — Do any of the members of your society take part in the prayer meeting simply by calling for a hymn? The remedy is in the hands of the leader or the prayer-meeting committee. At the opening of the meeting let the request be plainly made that in all such cases the member read the verse that especially appeals to him, or else give some testimony connected with the song called for.

When to Stop. — When the hour is up, and the hour has arrived for the evening meeting, — *stop!*

When the attendance is small, and every one present has evidently had his say, — *stop!*

When the meeting has been brought, by some strong testimony, to a fitting climax that will dwell in the memory, if it is near the time to close, introduce some form of concert testimony that will give utterance to those who have not yet taken part, and then — *stop!*

Without waiting for the pauses to lengthen, — *stop!*

Without giving a chance for restlessness and yawning, — *stop!*

Without scolding the members for failing to " occupy the time," — *stop!*

With no announcement that " there are just four minutes more," — which no one will be selfish enough to take, — *stop!*

With no preliminary nervous looking-up a closing hymn, and then looking around to see if any one is about to speak, and then looking for a better hymn and reconnoitring again, — *stop!*

With a few brisk words of encouragement, and a few reverent words of prayer, and a verse of a parting song, with the pastor's benediction, — *stop!*

But — if no meeting follows, and the members are

evidently eager to speak and eager to listen, — *don't* stop!

If there is one hesitant member, with whom you know the prayer-meeting committee is working to lead him into fuller expression, and if you think him on the point of taking part, though the rest are through, wait a minute, — *don't* stop!

If the impression of the meeting is deepening, — *don't* stop!

If souls are being born into the Kingdom, — *don't* stop!

If the visitors are getting restless, but the members are eager and interested, — *don't* stop!

With tact, with common sense, with a prayerful desire for the best, hold on, — *don't* stop!

Close It Effectively. — If a Christian Endeavor prayer meeting is well begun, half of its success is assured. If it is well ended, you have the other half. Do not close the meeting in a hurry, or, as one writer puts it, " like an army beating a retreat." Give yourself a plenty of time for a word or two at the end, driving home the main thought of the evening; also for the closing prayer and an appropriate closing song. A series of sentence prayers will be sure to send the members away with more thoughtfulness and devotion.

Do not exhaust in the early part of the evening all the novel features you have prepared. Save one for a surprise at the close. For example, you may have selected some hymn whose beautiful words are peculiarly appropriate to enforcing the theme of the evening. Ask the members to rise and read this hymn in concert, or alternating with you, verse about. Another method of closing is to unroll before the society a large sheet of paper upon which you have clearly printed some psalm or other passage of Scripture that will imprint the evening's lesson firmly upon the minds of the society. Hang this in clear sight, and call upon all to join you in repeating the passage.

Timing Them. — A Christian Endeavor prayer-meeting leader once got several of the Endeavorers from the "verse-reader's" class by main force. He did it in this way. At the opening of the meeting he quietly remarked, "Every member who gives a verse in this meeting will be expected to give a one-minute comment on it." Out then came the leader's watch, and with the first verse quoted the leader was ready to time the comment. "Good!" said the leader; "the first testimony was only ten seconds under time." The second testimony, however, brought up the society's credit, being twenty seconds over time. In this way the ice was broken, and the society discovered that it was possible to use the tongue as well as the heart in its meetings.

A Stratagem. — If a leader seriously objects to seeing before him many empty front seats, he may carry out the stratagem of a leader I once heard about, who, when the members failed to come forward, quietly took up his stand and walked to the back of the room, seated himself, and requested the audience to turn their chairs around facing him.

Thus those that were farthest in the rear found themselves occupying front seats!

No Back Seats! — One excellent way out of the vacant front-seat dilemma is to arrange the chairs in the form of a C. E. monogram, the leader seated opposite the opening in the C. Thus all members of the society are at almost equal distances from him.

Set Them to Work. — As I have suggested on a preceding page, as soon as possible after the new members join, before their enthusiasm has time to cool, the committee should get them to lead a meeting. Once settled to the work, they will not need any urging. The advantage of this point is apparent, and constitutes a strong objection to the plan of appointing leaders for more than one month ahead. Sometimes if the leaders are appointed so long a time ahead, it may be understood that a dual leadership may be established at any time, a new member being delegated to assist one of the appointed leaders in the conduct of the service.

Call for Them. — It is especially necessary that the prayer-meeting committee and the leader should co-operate. For instance, if the committee has asked several timid members to come prepared to offer a sentence prayer, let the leader be told of the plan, so that he may call for sentence prayers.

Notice the Stranger. — Be sure, leader, to get something for the stranger into every prayer meeting, — that is, if a single stranger is present. Say a word of welcome, privately and publicly. Invite all visiting Endeavorers to speak; much will thus be gained for the meeting. In your prayer mention the stranger within your gates. Introduce the strangers, before the meeting, to some one who will make them feel at home during the meeting, and after its close.

A Word to the Leader. — The members of the prayer-meeting committee should make it their especial duty to say a kind and appreciative word to the leader after the close of the meeting. If he is timid and a beginner, he probably feels that he has made a failure of the meeting, and a word of praise will save him from a world of despondency, and add greatly to his future zeal and efficiency.

A Word of Encouragement. — The leader can do much to help the timid members. A word from him will assist even those most tied down to the " verse-readers' class " to escape from their bondage. After a verse from the Bible has been timidly quoted, let the leader say a few words to bring out the beauty of the verse and its appropriateness to the topic of the evening. Sometimes the leader may ask a question concerning the verse, letting any one answer that will. When a sentence or two is hesitatingly added to the verse thus given, the leader should not delay giving his approval to the thought, if only by a few words. Our members will be far more ready to "take the next step" if the step they have already taken meets with a word of praise.

CHAPTER VII.

PRAYER IN THE MEETINGS.

A Good Prayer. — Many of our Endeavorers are learning what it is, and are putting that knowledge in practice for the good of their fellow members. Many more need to learn.

In the first place, a good prayer is the expression of one's real being. It never springs from the brain merely, but from the life. The one who is praying a good prayer never thinks what others are thinking about his prayer. He forgets that others are listening, and remembers only that he is talking with God.

A good prayer, therefore, simply asks for things the one who prays eagerly desires, confesses things for which he is truly sorrowful, or praises God for things for which he is sincerely grateful. The petition, confession, and gratitude will be in the prayer solely because they have first been in the life.

It follows, of course, that a good prayer will be very simple. When one asks a favor of one very dear to him, he does not use long sentences or long words. When one confesses a sin to men, he puts it as concisely as possible. When one says, " Thank you," to a friend, it is not with a set speech. Pompous prayers, wordy prayers, affected prayers, are insincere prayers.

If your heart is really touched by any need or sorrow of your brother's, you can make a good prayer. If you are truly striving to rid yourself of any sin, you can make a good prayer. If your heart is running over with gratitude to God for any blessing, you can make a good prayer.

It may not be more than a sentence long. It may be spoken in a voice so low as to be heard only a few feet away, and so trembling as to be unintelligible to those who hear, but it will be a good prayer. God owns it, and human souls will own it, too.

And if you can make a good prayer, it is your duty to do so.

An Opening Prayer. — Many societies will find it helpful if the members should commit to memory some such prayer as the following, which is regularly repeated in concert by the members of a certain Australian society at the opening of every Christian Endeavor meeting:

"Heavenly Father, draw near to us as we now draw near to thee. Mercifully grant that thy Holy Spirit may in all things direct and rule our hearts, and renew us in the spirit of our minds. Deliver us from all sloth in thy work, all coldness in thy cause, and grant that by looking unto thee we may rekindle our love, and by waiting upon thee may renew our strength, through Jesus Christ, our Lord. Amen."

Not a few of the psalms will furnish appropriate passages for the introduction of the service.

A Prayer Meeting. — A meeting entirely devoted to prayer with the exception of singing, the songs

PRAYER IN THE MEETINGS. 85

themselves being prayer songs, will do much to bring the society into the spirit of prayer, and introduce more prayers into the coming meetings.

It must be understood beforehand that the one method of participation in this meeting will be by prayer. Sentence prayers should be called for several times, and definite topics of prayer should be proposed at different times in the evening, such as prayer for associate members, for the church and its work, for the pastor, for missions, for the temperance cause, for the Sunday school, for the Christian Endeavor committees.

The concert repetition of prayers from the Bible that may be written on the blackboard or printed on large sheets of manilla paper will be helpful, as will also be the reading in concert of some prayer poem or hymn. Of course the members of the society will feel free to take part more than once if there is opportunity.

Two Good Plans. — An excellent way to get members to take part in prayer is to give them slips of paper bearing appropriate topics for prayer, and ask the member to make use of them. Another way is to suggest that the member select a verse of Scripture, repeat it, and then try to follow it with a brief prayer suggested by the quotation. It is a good plan for those who find difficulty in praying in public always to pray out loud when they pray at home.

Praying a Psalm. — Endeavorers frequently in their meetings repeat psalms in concert, or sing psalms, chanting them or otherwise; but why should they not use the prayer psalms as their own prayers? There are several ways of doing this. One of the best is to get the members to commit to memory these priceless portions of Scripture. In that case, all heads can be bowed and the psalm repeated in concert.

Another method requires all members to come to the meeting with copies of the Bible. This is eminently desirable for many other reasons. Opening their Bibles to the prayer psalm, let all the Endeavorers kneel and read the psalm in concert. Still another method prescribes that, while the members are kneeling, the Endeavorers of a certain row shall read the psalm aloud, taking it verse about, in order.

What is a Chain Prayer? — Here is a definition of a chain prayer given by an Australian paper. Few of our societies can come up to its requirements, and yet it is an admirable definition to work toward: "A chain prayer is one in which *every active* member of the society present takes part. It is started by the leader, taken up by the next, and so on around, no one concluding with "for Christ's sake, Amen," until it reaches the leader again, who thus closes it. Each petition should be but a sentence, and an endeavor should be made to make it harmonize with the others, and embody the special subject of the chain prayer, which should never be but for some specific and definite thing. Now, then, try again."

Special Subjects. — When you have sentence prayers in your society you will find it exceedingly helpful to propose definite subjects for prayer, and these subjects may well be connected with the theme of the evening or with some testimony that has immediately preceded.

Silent Prayer. — One of the most useful exercises of the prayer meeting is silent prayer. To render it helpful, however, it should be introduced, not in a mechanical, but in a very appropriate, way. It should come at the climax of the meeting, and should emphasize the principal point of the evening's discussion.

The leader should always propose some theme for the silent prayer, applying the chief thought of the evening to the consciences and individual lives of those before him. If, for example, the meeting has been one of thanksgiving, during a moment of silent prayer at the close let the Endeavorers give thanks to God for some definite blessings of their lives. If the meeting has taken an evangelistic turn, has been directed perhaps to the winning of the associate members and the non-Christians, during a moment's silent prayer let all Christian hearts rise in earnest petition for the salvation of the souls that are dear to them, and while all heads are bowed, let an opportunity be given for any to rise that may wish to signify their desire to enter upon the Christian life.

It is a common mistake to close too abruptly this season of silent prayer. A full minute is none too long. Often the leader breaks the silent prayer before many in the audience have fairly begun to pray. It is customary to request some Endeavorer to close the silent prayer with a few words of vocal prayer, and careful selection should be made of the person who is to take up the responsible task of putting into words and carrying to a higher level the secret petitions of so many.

Kneeling in Prayer. — Some societies have the custom of kneeling while sentence prayers or long prayers are being offered. This is exceedingly helpful, at least for occasional use. It will be found that many will take part in public prayer when they are kneeling that would not under other circumstances. It is an excellent plan, before the members rise from their knees, to sing softly some verse of a prayer hymn, such as "Nearer my God to thee," or "Take my life, and let it be Consecrated, Lord, to thee."

Concerted Prayer. — It will be helpful if all members of the prayer-meeting committee agree, no matter where they are or what they may be doing, to offer concerted prayer, say at the noon hour, for the society to which they belong, and for the special work their committee is endeavoring to do.

Pray for Each. — Definite prayer is the only prayer that has power. It is a good thing for the prayer-meeting committee to meet regularly for the purpose of prayer for the members of the society by name, with a roll of the society open before them. Prayer should be offered by each person in turn, according to the needs of that particular person.

Prayer Circle. — Christ's promise regarding the two or three met together in his name may be claimed without a formal meeting, by what has been termed a "prayer circle." This consists of three or more Endeavorers who agree to pray for some common purpose. It may be for the salvation of some mutual friend. Whatever it is, the subject of the prayer is kept a secret. A fixed time each day is set for the prayer, which is offered wherever the Endeavorers may happen to be, and until the prayer is answered the Endeavorers constantly raise it. When their petition is granted, report is made to the society. No names are mentioned, unless such mention is thought best for some special reason. The society is simply asked to join with the prayer circle in thanksgiving for another answered prayer.

Prayer Trios. — If there are those in the society that find it difficult to pray in Christian Endeavor meetings, the committee may form prayer trios. The members of these agree to pray consecutively in the coming meeting. The central one of each trio is to be a member that has never before prayed in public. The prayers that come before and after his should of course be brief and simple, so as to give him confidence.

A Prayer Class. — Some pastors organize among their Endeavorers what are called prayer classes, — little meetings for the gaining of fervency and ease in public prayer. One pastor hung up in the place where this class met, a placard bearing these words:

> Heavenly Father,
> Teach us to pray.
> For Christ's sake. Amen.

Those who wished to learn to pray were asked to use the first two and the last lines of the placard, supplying a sentence or two in the middle.

A Week of Prayer. — I have heard of a society whose meetings were languishing, that adopted the wise and vigorous method of holding a week of prayer regarding the matter. The society met every night, and engaged in earnest prayer and consultation for the sole purpose of advancing their spiritual life.

The Prayer Chain. — The World's Christian Endeavor Prayer Chain should be utilized in our meetings, even though not all the members of the society may be links of the chain. The general theme of prayer for the month should be introduced in each meeting, and sometimes it will add to the spiritual tone of the meeting if some Endeavorer reads the special requests for prayer for the week and if these are remembered in brief sentence prayers by the members. The links of the Prayer Chain in your society may constitute themselves an informal committee to carry out these suggestions.

Birthday Prayers. — Young People's Christian Endeavor societies might make very much more than is made of the birthdays of their members. The Juniors in this matter are far ahead of their seniors. It would not be out of the way to appoint a birthday committee, that should keep on record all the birthdays of all the members of the society. At each meeting this committee should announce the birthdays which will fall during the coming week, and during that week those members are especially remembered in prayer by all the society. If it is not thought best to appoint this birthday committee, this work may be assumed by the prayer-meeting committee.

A Petition Book. — Some societies have found it an advantage to open a petition book, accessible to all members of the society. On one page will be entered the various prayers the members of the society are especially anxious to have answered, and on the opposite page a space is left vacant for a statement in regard to the answer, when it comes, and how. Such a book as this, though it may at first sight seem mechanical, has furnished convincing proof that God does hear and answer prayer.

CHAPTER VIII.

USING THE BIBLE.

Bring Your Bibles. — A good work for the prayer-meeting committee to undertake will be to get the Endeavorers to make it a practice to bring their Bibles to the prayer meeting. Frequently in the progress of the meeting there are opportunities for the recitation of appropriate Scripture. This your memories may not retain, but if you have your Bibles, you can turn to them and use them.

Concert and responsive readings from the Bible would become much more general if members would bring their Bibles. Such readings are frequently proposed in the published commentaries on the topic, and they are always very helpful.

Endeavorers should enjoy the companionship of the Book, and should be glad to have it with them, even if they do not open it. A few moments of Bible-reading while we are waiting for the meeting to begin is the best preparation for the meeting.

Besides, in the course of the meeting, helpful comments on Bible passages will be given. If the Endeavorers know how to mark their Bibles wisely, they will want them at hand to mark. And for the final reason, the Bible carried along the street is a sort of Christian banner, and every Christian

Endeavorer should wish to show his colors. In this commendable practice of carrying the Bible to the prayer meeting the prayer-meeting committee should take the lead, and urge it by precept as well, until the other members have taken up the custom.

Name the Reference. — One method of alluring Endeavorers from the verse-readers' class is to urge them to name the reference before they repeat it. It adds much to the interest of a Bible quotation to know who said it and from what part of the Bible it comes. Besides, this will be a step in the direction of more original participation.

A Chain of Verses. — The prayer-meeting committee will obtain a large number of slips of writing paper of different colors, and will place upon each a Bible reference. These are to be given to the Endeavorers to take home. Each is to find his verse, write it upon the slip, commit it to memory, and bring the slip to the next meeting.

At this meeting all the members rise in turn, and read — or better, recite — their verses. They then give the slip of paper to the chairman of the prayer-meeting committee or to the leader, who forms them into a chain. This chain, being sent to a hospital, will be enjoyed by the patients.

An Initial Meeting. — Ask the members to choose Bible texts beginning with the initials of their names, and repeat them at the next meeting, giving the reasons why they selected those texts, and why they should like to have them for the mottoes of their lives.

Bringing in the Sunday-school Lesson. — For a good many years, the prayer-meeting topics have been in line with the Sunday-school lessons. The Christian Endeavor topics are never the same as those of the Sunday school, but are usually derived from them. This fact makes it especially fitting that the Christian Endeavor prayer meeting should take thought regarding the Sunday-school lesson that usually precedes it.

One of the best ways of taking part in the Christian Endeavor meeting is to speak of the thought that has most impressed one in the Sunday-school class discussions. This effects a double end: it advertises the Sunday school and encourages the teachers, and at the same time it enriches the Christian Endeavor prayer meeting. The prayer-meeting committee should occasionally advise the leader to call for these reminiscences of the Sunday-school lesson. Some may think that this way of participating in the prayer meeting will cause it to become monotonous, and to seem a mere repetition of the Sunday school; but this is far from being the case. The truths taught in the Sunday school are fixed upon the memory, and at the same time new light is thrown upon them.

Bible Characters. — An interesting prayer meeting is one whose central idea is Bible characters. One Endeavorer, for instance, may read a paper on Miriam or Ruth, a second may treat Balaam or Peter, a third may give an essay on Timothy as a Christian Endeavor worker, and so on.

A Psalm at the Start. — No Christian Endeavor society is well equipped for its work unless the memories of its members contain a repertoire of the psalms, especially those most suited to responsive exercises. One of the best ways of opening a prayer meeting is by the concert repetition of one of these psalms. This mode of opening always gives a tone of spirituality to the meeting. Frequently, too, such psalms make a most fitting close for the meeting.

A Psalm Meeting. — Once a year an entire meeting might well be devoted to the psalms. Following any good commentary on the psalms, assign to different members different classes of these inspired hymns, as, to one the psalms of petition, to another those of praise, to another the Messianic psalms, to a fifth the imprecatory psalms. Psalms with special histories, connected with prominent events in the life of David or of the nation, should be assigned to separate members.

One Endeavorer might speak of the psalms that have had important influence upon the great men of the earth at the different crises of their history. Another might show how often the psalms are quoted in the New Testament. Another might show the influence of the psalms on our modern hymns, many of which are simply paraphrases.

Of course the singing of the psalms and the concert repetition of them from memory or otherwise will form one of the principal features of the evening. The members may also be asked to name their favorite psalms, telling why they are especially dear to them.

A Bible-Reading. — A capital plan to get the members well started in a meeting is this: Let the leader at the opening announce rapidly the places of half a dozen texts. As each reference is announced let some Endeavorer repeat it after the leader, thus volunteering to look up the passage in the Bible. These members will hold themselves ready to read the passages when the reader comes to need them in the course of his remarks.

The Opening Bible-Reading. — Prayer-meeting leaders should not uniformly read, themselves, the Bible passage selected as basis for the thought of the evening. Sometimes let them call upon the members to repeat Bible verses bearing upon the subject, — this to take the place of the selection for the evening. Sometimes one of the psalms may be repeated in concert, or the leader and society may alternate, verse about; or the psalm may be repeated by the young men and the young women of the audience, they alternating the verses.

Sometimes the introductory passage may be written upon a blackboard, or a large sheet of paper, so plainly that the audience can read it and repeat it together. Many of the Scripture selections for the meetings are suitable for recitations, and a good speaker, other than the leader, should be instructed beforehand to commit them to memory and repeat them, coming in front of the society; or the leader himself may repeat the introductory Scripture.

Where the authorized and the revised versions of the passage for the evening vary conspicuously, it will be interesting for the leader to read one verse in the authorized version, while another Endeavorer follows with the same verse from the revised version, and so on with the rest of the selection.

Bible Reference Meetings. — To carry on a meeting of this character, get the members each of them to select a passage from the Bible, preferably one that is not in common use, that illustrates the topic of the evening. These references, written on slips of paper, are to be handed to the prayer-meeting committee several days before the meeting. The committee arranges them according to a plan the leader will form, and at the opening of the meeting the slips are handed out to the members, numbered. They are to be read in the order of the numbers, the leader joining them together by helpful remarks. In the latter service he may be assisted by some of the Endeavorers.

A Bible Meeting. — For this meeting let the leader select a certain chapter of the Bible and make the Endeavorers promise to read this chapter during the coming week, and present at the next meeting, each one, some thought suggested by the chapter. A similar meeting might well be built up on the daily readings of the week.

A Favorite Text Meeting. — Ask the members one week beforehand to come prepared at the next meeting to give, each of them, his favorite Bible text, combining the recitation of it with a few words telling why it is especially precious to him. The pastor should be notified of the plan beforehand, and should be present to speak at the close of the meeting upon the lessons that should be brought out. He will especially notice what texts are the favorites of the greatest number, as many will doubtless light upon the same passages.

Bible-Reading. — The prayer meetings are not to vie with the Sunday school in the matter of Bible study, and yet they can be exceedingly helpful in this line, and the prayer-meeting committee may direct such studies. For one thing, insist upon the daily readings. Call for reports occasionally, endeavoring to find out how many of the members are making actual daily use of these readings. Once in a while appoint six members to speak at the next meeting, taking thoughts, each of them, from the daily reading of one of the days.

Sometimes let the prayer-meeting committee select a chapter of the Bible especially full of thoughts regarding the coming topic, and request each member of the society to read this chapter before the next meeting.

It may be thought advisable, in some societies, to enter upon more systematic work. One society I have heard of appoints for each day of the week one chapter in the Old, and one in the New, Testament, and calls for little talks at the weekly meetings, based upon these chapters.

If this is not needed, it is well sometimes to announce special Bible-readings, whose fruits are to be gathered up in the coming prayer meeting. During one week, for example, the members might be asked to read the accounts of all of Christ's healings of the blind, or of the three cases in which Christ raised people from death, or the whole of the Sermon on the Mount, or all of Solomon's proverbs regarding wisdom, or the entire book of Ecclesiastes. or the Messianic prophecies of Isaiah, or the seven most prominent parables of Christ's, or the last three chapters of Revelation. A pleasant exercise would be a ten minutes' review of this Bible-reading, chiefly in the form of questions presented to the society by a bright speaker.

Special Bible Study. — Not for a regular, but for an occasional, feature of the work, it would help the society and add to the prayer meeting if the members should meet every week for an hour, and study the Bible under the lead of some wide-awake Bible student, having in special view the needs of the Christian Endeavor society.

The best plan would be to study the Bible topically, a course not pursued by the Sunday school. In one meeting, for example, the Endeavorers might collate Bible passages upon prayer, and try to find out what the Bible doctrine regarding prayer really is. Sin, salvation, happiness, forgiveness, are samples of the topics that might be discussed. Such a class as this would speedily lead to a more frequent and wise use of the Bible in the Christian Endeavor prayer meeting.

CHAPTER IX.

EMPHASIZE THE PLEDGE.

A Special Pledge. — One prayer-meeting committee of which I have heard is so firm a believer in pledges, and so deeply conscious of the requirements of its own work, that its members take a special additional pledge of their own. They promise in this pledge to make the most of their opportunities for deepening the spiritual life of every member placed in their charge, and to do the best they can for the improvement of the weekly prayer meeting of the society.

A Pledge Meeting. — Meetings based on the Christian Endeavor pledge should be held at least once a year, and the uniform topics always provide for such a meeting. It is a good plan to divide the pledge into sections, appointing one member of the society to treat each section. At this meeting, of course, the pledge should be repeated in concert. A versified form of the pledge may be sung. The United Society of Christian Endeavor furnishes an interesting Bible-reading on the pledge. A chart containing some novel arrangement of the pledge might be placed before the society; some such arrangement, for instance, as the following, prepared by Rev. W. H. G. Temple:

OUR PLEDGE.

The distinctive feature of the Christian Endeavor
movement, to which we have all given our
loyal assent, and by which we
have promised to
stand,

PROVIDES FOR

DAILY DEVOTION.

I promise . . . to pray and read the Bible every
day.

WEEKLY TESTIMONY.

To be present at and to take some part, aside from
singing, in every Christian Endeavor
prayer meeting.

MONTHLY CONSECRATION.

And, if obliged to be absent from the monthly consecration meeting, to send, if possible, at least
a verse of Scripture to be read in response to my name at the
roll-call.

CONSTANT LOYALTY TO CHURCH AND CAUSE.

To do my duty, support, and attend regularly the
Sunday and midweek services
of my church.

DOING ALL

In the name and strength of . . .
. . . the Lord Jesus Christ.
BY FAITH. AMEN.

A pledge question-box would furnish an interesting feature of the evening. To this question-box the members will contribute questions regarding the difficulties each has met in attempting to keep the pledge. The leader will answer some of the questions himself, and refer others for answer to the pastor and the more shrewd among the Endeavorers.

A pledge open parliament might well be carried on, with such a topic as, "How does the pledge help you in your daily living?" or, "What part of the pledge do you find most difficult to keep, and why?" or, "Why should every Christian be willing to take the Christian Endeavor pledge?" A pledge meeting should by no means lack the element of prayer, for we greatly need wisdom to teach us all that the pledge implies, and strength to accomplish the things we have pledged ourselves to do.

Records of Participation. — Few methods of spurring a lagging society are better than the following: Let the prayer-meeting committee keep a record every week for a month of the mode which each Endeavorer takes of participating in the meetings. At the end of the month, let a copy of his record be sent to each member, while the record as a whole is read before the society, names, of course, being omitted. If this is kept up for several months in succession, improvements being commended publicly and privately, with here and there a word of exhortation, the gain will be immediate and marked. It will not be necessary to follow this plan indefinitely.

Prayer-meeting Committee Blanks. — The following prayer-meeting committee blank is used by a society in Washington, D.C. The tally is not kept by names. The members of the committee take turns in filling out the weekly report. These reports are preserved, and serve as material for the monthly and term reports of the committee.

REPORT OF PRAYER-MEETING COMMITTEE.

For July 10, 1892.

Number of Persons Present, 33 $\begin{cases} \text{Active,} & 13 \\ \text{Associate,} & 9 \\ \text{Visiting,} & 11 \end{cases}$

PERSONS PARTICIPATING.

Active Members	// × /////// × /////	= 15
Associate Members	////////	= 8
Others		= 1

"×" means participating by proxy.   Total, 24

CARLETON E. SNELL,
Member of the Prayer-Meeting Committee.

It will even prove stimulating to keep in the same way a separate report for each person. These reports should not, of course, be made public, but copies of them should be handed to each member. At the close of the month they will show not only how many times he has been present and taken part, but in what way he has taken part. The committee, for example, might use the letter T for "testimony,"

B for "Bible verses," P for "prayer," etc. Such a definite account would be of great use to the committee in enabling them to lay their hands upon the weak spots in the society.

A Spur. — The best of societies occasionally becomes sluggish, and needs a reminder of the pledge the members have taken, and a stimulus to renewed exertions. Some such circular as the following, whose author is Rev. W. H. G. Temple, if prepared to meet the special need of the society and scattered broadcast among the members by print or manifolder, could hardly help stirring them up to fresh energy and zeal.

Dear Endeavorer: With what spirit do you propose to begin this five months' work in our society? Ought we not individually to take an inventory of our motives, and find out just where we stand? Let us ask ourselves these questions:

1. Do we intend conscientiously to keep our pledge?
2. Do we intend to do just enough to clear ourselves from condemnation, or do we propose to start out to be true-hearted and whole-hearted?
3. Can we be counted on to make our committees efficient, and to personally show constant growth in service?
4. Are we willing to commit ourselves to the very best answers we can give to these questions?

Please remember that the work of your prayer-meeting committee will be an utter failure without God's blessing and your individual support. We promise our most enthusiastic efforts, if you will stand by us. In order to get an expression of your willingness to co-operate, we ask you to sign and detach the subjoining coupon, and return the same promptly to us.

Enclosed please find booklet containing our topics and daily readings,

> Yours affectionately,
> for Christ and the church,
> THE PRAYER-MEETING COMMITTEE.

Detach, and return, signed, to the prayer-meeting committee.

I hereby confirm my loyalty to our Christian Endeavor pledge, and promise to do all I can, whether on a committee or not, to advance the interests of our society during the next five months.

....

To Keep the Pledge. — Whenever the prayer-meeting committee takes up some special plan for the meeting, great care should be taken that the members have some opportunity to keep their pledge by taking part in concert. In this way the pledge idea is emphasized, and the concert feature may at the same time be made one of the most helpful and inspiring features of the evening.

For instance, at the opening of a question-box meeting of a certain society the audience were requested to rise and to read responsively with the leader that well-known question hymn, "Art thou weary, art thou languid?" the leader repeating the first two lines of each stanza and the audience repeating in concert the answer, — the second two lines. This exercise was appropriately closed by the repetition of a prayer-hymn in the same hymn-book, in which the leader and audience joined.

Instead of this hymn exercise it is well occasionally to have the audience repeat some passage of Scripture that all may be supposed to know, such as the Beatitudes, the Lord's Prayer, a portion of the first chapter of John, the twenty-third, forty-second, fifty-first, thirty-fourth, twenty-fourth or nineteenth psalm. If the leader wishes to use some unfamiliar passage of Scripture, a copy of it should be placed before the audience, written plainly on a blackboard or on a large sheet of manilla paper.

CHAPTER X.

THE MUSIC.

Monotony in Opening. — Many Christian Endeavor societies make the mistake of opening their meetings always in the same way. This strikes the keynote of monotony at the very beginning. If a novel introduction is planned, the meeting is not likely to run in the old ruts. Especially is this warning needed with reference to the opening song service.

It is an admirable plan, once in a while, to sing at the opening five or six songs, until the Endeavorers have reached a high pitch of spiritual enthusiasm and devotion. If this plan, however, is uniformly pursued, it will ultimately fail of the desired effect. More than that, the members will come to think that the meeting is not begun until the close of the song service, and with this plea will excuse themselves for frequent tardiness. One of the very best introductions to a Christian Endeavor meeting is a season of prayer without any singing at all, and this mode of introduction should be used quite as frequently as the introductory praise service.

The Organist. — I often think that an organist can do more for the success of the prayer-meeting than the leader himself. Spirited, sympathetic playing leads to singing of the same kind. The model organist will never race ahead of the audience, no matter how pokily they sing, but will gradually lead them to greater promptness. The model organist will play a prelude for only the most unfamiliar hymns. All the familiar hymns will be sung to the chord alone. There will be, of course, no interludes between the verses. They are an impertinence.

The model organist will keep her seat at the instrument during the meeting, that no time may be lost after a hymn is called for. She will pay strict attention to the number of the hymn and the number of the verses requested. If the announcement is made in a low voice, she will not guess at the number, but call for a repetition of the announcement.

The work of organist is arduous, and if your society possesses more than one competent person, you should by all means arrange for rotation in office. In my own society six take turns at this pleasant task.

A Hymn Leader. — If your society has timid members, — and what society has not? — you may find it a good plan to accustom them to leadership by appointing for each meeting a hymn leader, whose sole work will be the selection of hymns and the announcement of them. He will sit facing the society, with the other leader.

Rapid Singing. — American congregational singing, for some reason or other, is noted for its slowness. That it is too slow, you can easily convince yourself by timing the singing of a stanza, and then trying to read the same stanza in the same time. The necessary drawing out of the words would effectually hide whatever meaning they might otherwise convey. We have been droning out our hymns for so long that the method has almost become sacred to our minds, and a sense of levity attaches itself to a more rational mode of singing.

Nevertheless, our societies will find it very advantageous if they can increase the rapidity of their singing to such a degree that the thought of the hymns can be gathered much as if the hymn were read. An Australian audience would sing four hymns while an American audience is singing one, and the spirit and effectiveness of their singing, the unanimity with which their congregations change the volume from soft to loud or the reverse, and the rapidity from fast to slow or from slow to rapid, are proofs of the value of a more brisk rendition of gospel hymns.

Reading Hymns. — The custom is extending of reading hymns occasionally in concert, instead of singing them. It is a custom greatly to be commended. In this way a hymn takes less time than if it were sung, and the thought of the hymn is brought out as, in our ordinary way of singing, it never is. A series of hymns thus read in concert will prove a very effective exercise.

Hymns Impromptu. — I know of nothing, except chain prayers, that will add more to the zest of a meeting than the impromptu starting of hymns without any announcement whatever. In every society, with a little practice and determination, this great aid to a spiritual meeting can be obtained. If you have no one person that is willing to undertake the work, you can easily find two that will sit together and start the hymns impromptu, supporting one another.

A Hymn a Month. — Your society should adopt a society hymn, expressive of the particular aims of your work. In addition to this, many societies have found it a pleasant custom to commit to memory one hymn a month. Our memories contain too few hymns. Many are familiar to us to the extent of their first stanza, but with the second we stumble, and with the third we are utterly at a loss. These memory hymns are to be introduced at each meeting, and are to be sung without the book.

Explore the Hymn-Books. — Our hymn-books are not half used. If you have no music committee, the prayer-meeting committee should make it its business to go over all the songs in your hymn-book and introduce the society to those that are unfamiliar, at the first convenient opportunity. For this purpose, some societies permit the prayer-meeting or the music committee to select the hymns. Otherwise, these committees should request the leader to call for the hymns they wish to introduce.

Choir Testimony. — If your society has that useful adjunct, a Christian Endeavor choir, occasionally get them to give united testimony, by rising and singing two or three verses of some appropriate hymn. After this, each one will give his thoughts on the subject of the hymn. Close the testimony by singing together the last verse of the hymn. If you have no choir, these exercises may be carried out by half a dozen picked Endeavorers.

A Hymn Prayer Meeting. — A great variety of hymn prayer meetings is possible. The meeting may be based upon the life and writings of a single author. An evening with Fanny Crosby, or with Frances Ridley Havergal, or Watts, or Charles Wesley, could not fail to be filled with the greatest profit and delight. The noble lives of these Christian poets, and the exalted sentiments of their works, would furnish a rich evening.

Some one should read a brief biography of the life of the writer, or it may be divided into several portions, each assigned to one Endeavorer. Interspersed among the exercises of the evening should be the most important hymns written by the author. There should be prayers and testimonies based upon these hymns, or upon any others the Endeavorers may wish to speak about.

A general hymn meeting, in which each Endeavorer tells his favorite hymn, or gives some incidents regarding the hymn and the good it has done in exceptional circumstances, is another admirable plan. Such books as Hezekiah Butterworth's "Story of the Hymns," and Dr. Robinson's "Annotations on Popular Hymns," would be of the greatest assistance in planning a meeting of this character.

A Hymn Service. — The week before, present to each Endeavorer a slip of paper containing the following questions, with blanks for written replies:

"Name your favorite hymn."
"Why do you like it?"
"How has it helped you?"
"What can you tell about the author and the history of the hymn?"

Let it be understood that these questions may be answered wholly or in part; that the answers may be read by the writers or handed to the leader of the meeting for him to read; and that, if the members desire, they may give their answers orally instead of writing them. Occasionally in the course of the meeting let the hymns be sung after they are mentioned by the participants. At the close of the meeting have the leader, or some ready speaker, sum up the entire meeting in its prominent features, especially recounting the hymns that have most frequently been mentioned as helpful, and the reasons for the helpfulness of hymns that have most often been named.

A Few More Points. — Many hymns, especially those that are in the form of prayers, should be sung with bowed heads. — A meeting, possibly once a year, may be devoted to the hymn-book, singing it through for the purpose of becoming familiar with the hymns less commonly used. If your song book has not a topical index, it will greatly add to your efficiency as a prayer-meeting worker if you make one for yourself, pasting it in your own book, and giving copies of it to others. — If your music committee organizes a Christian Endeavor choir, the choir should part of the time sit together in the front of the audience, and part of the time its members should be scattered throughout the room. — It is a pleasant plan occasionally at the opening of the meeting to mingle song with the reading of the Scripture, a few verses being followed by an appropriate hymn, after which a few more verses are read and another hymn is sung, and so on. — If you want to emphasize a hymn, have the audience rise while singing it. Any audience will sing better standing. — Another way to emphasize a song is to ask the members, after they have sung a stanza, to read it together in concert, or to sing it once more, or to sing the chorus a second time. The second singing will always be more hearty than the first. — A good way to introduce novelty into the singing of a hymn is to ask for a reading of the verses by the members, each verse being read by a different member before it is sung. — Occasionally let the leader call for the singing of a hymn, the verses in unison and the chorus in parts. Hymns of moderate range are almost always more effective when sung in unison. — Sometimes it is well to ask the young women of the society to sing one verse, the young men the next; or the young women the stanzas, the young men joining in the chorus; or the audience may be divided, the left section singing one stanza, the right the second, and all joining in the third. Wherever the hymn consists of question and answer, or is divided in similarly suggestive ways, the leader should get different portions of the audience to sing these different parts.

CHAPTER XI.

POINTS FOR GOOD MEETINGS.

Standing While Speaking. — Few things will help a prayer meeting more than the habit of standing while taking part in the meeting, whether to pray or to testify. The prayer-meeting committee should, whenever opportunity offers, urge this custom upon the society. The timid will object to it, but will find, on trying it, that standing is one of the best ways of overcoming timidity.

Every one, especially after a little practice, can think better upon his feet; and even if he does not think better, what he says sounds better and makes more impression. At first only one or two may rise, and they may seem unduly conspicuous, but after a while others will be sure to join in. Urge upon the members that by rising they show that they are not ashamed to testify for Christ; and bring forward the common-sense argument that they can be heard with twice the ease, though they speak with only one-half the force.

Besides, every Christian Endeavorer should train himself to take part, if need be, in large assemblies; and speakers in such gatherings must rise to their feet. There is the slight additional argument, that when two or more start to speak simultaneously, if they rise, the leader can easily indicate which is to have precedence; but this is not so easy when they remain seated.

Cut it Short! — There is one thing that the Christian Endeavor movement may have confident hope of accomplishing, and that is a shortening of the speeches made in prayer meeting by the present and all following generations. Here is a church whose prayer meetings are attended by, say, one hundred and twenty persons. Forty of these are men. Five of these men are in the habit of speaking at every meeting when they are present; and they never speak less than ten minutes. The result, a dead prayer meeting, and a dying church. In the first place, there should be at least twenty prayers and testimonies in every prayer meeting thus well attended. There should be twenty more in the next prayer meeting. And, as a rule, — with, of course, occasional exceptions, — one who has spoken at length in one meeting should take but brief part in the next meeting.

It is absolutely wrong for any church to be satisfied with the participation in prayer meeting of only an insignificant fraction of the congregation. "Why, Brother So-and-so always speaks so well, and I like to hear him. So do we all. Why not give him his ten minutes every evening, and we keep still?" Why not? Because Brother So-and-so will not live forever, and others should be training to take his place. Because in multitude of counsellors there is safety. Because *your* life has a lesson and a message for other lives. Because for your growth it is necessary that you express before others the best that is in you. Because from many voices raised in prayer and testimony there is an inspiration that a few cannot give, it matters not how eloquent and able may be the words they say.

Endeavorers believe this. Their **pledge** binds them to take some part in every meeting. The large number of members compels each one to be brief. And who is the loser? Nay, who is not the gainer?

Believe us, Endeavorers, two earnest sentences, pulsing with thought and feeling, having back of them many an hour of prayer and life, fired with a plain, ardent purpose hot from your heart, will reach other hearts as twenty-two sentences would not. Learn the art of condensing. Learn the art of selection. Don't think it necessary to say all you know at one time. Other evenings are coming. Don't think it necessary to say all you know on any one subject. Others are to speak after you. Be modest, and sensible, and — cut it short!

Things Timidity Spoils. — If timid people only stopped to think how their timidity hinders God's work, they would cease to be complacent toward it, and would drive it from their lives, gaining instead that " holy boldness " which Christ gives to all who put their trust in him, and which enables even the most bashful of his children to do whatever work he has set before them.

You have a striking experience, the recital of which would cheer and comfort many a soul, but — you are too timid. You have a strong influence over that erring brother, and a word from you might bring him back to honor and duty, but — you are too timid. You have a deep reverence for the Bible, and your apt quotations from its rich pages would bless all who listen, but — you are too timid. Your prayers in your closet uplift and strengthen you as in public they would uplift and strengthen others, but — you are too timid.

O what wretched worms we are to fear to say a few earnest words to one another about this great business of our living! O what unworthy children of the King, we who are afraid to talk to our Father in the presence of our brothers and sisters! How feeble is our trust in God, how miserably strong is our egotistic fear for ourselves, and for the impression we may or may not make on others!

Let us all hear God saying to us, as he said to Moses: "Who hath made man's mouth? Have not I, the Lord? Now therefore go, and I will be with thy mouth and teach thee what thou shalt say."

A Few Hints to the Timid. — You have something to say; we will take that for granted. If not, get something to say.

Being timid, you should take part as soon in the meeting as possible, that the meeting may not be spoiled for you by your dread of taking part. As your timidity wears off, your participation may move backward in the meeting hour.

If you take part early in the meeting, you will not be likely to be embarrassed by hearing some one else begin at the same time you do.

When that occurs, however, turn to the person who has begun to speak, and nod to him or her, implying that you give way. Then, after he or she has finished, be sure to speak next, for every one will expect you to.

One of the best ways of overcoming timidity is to rise when you speak. This puts one on his mettle, and rallies all his forces. Try it.

Begin to speak *while* you are rising, and there will then be no danger of hearing some one start to testify as soon as you have gained your feet.

Speak in a voice as even and firm and decided as you can command. The voice you assume has an important influence on your feelings. If you can make your voice courageous, you will soon become so yourself.

Do not speak too rapidly. You will thus lose self-control, and, what is worse, no one will get much good out of what you are saying.

Do not be disconcerted if you cannot remember the rest of what you were going to say. Just stop. If *you* cannot remember it, probably *they* would not remember it, either.

Don't be afraid of your fellow-Endeavorers. Argue thus with yourself: "I should not be afraid to say this to Mary Brown, should I? No. Or to Will Lemons? No." And so you may go on through the whole society. Then, if you would not be afraid to say it to any of these separately, why should you be afraid to say it to all of them together?

Go into a meeting with the determination to speak

boldly for Christ. Say to yourself, "Now I am going to say this thing, and I am not going to have any foolishness about it. If it is to be said, why should I wait and be miserable worrying over it? Out with it at once!"

Remember, above all things, that you are not speaking for yourself, but for God, and he will see that you speak to his glory. You have Christ's plain word for it. Is not that enough?

Stick to the Prayer Meeting. — Once in a while I hear of a society that drops its regular prayer meeting for the purpose of listening to some lecture. To be sure, the lecture is always on some religious subject, and the speaker is one especially invited by the society. The members are present in large numbers; and yet I am certain that such meetings are a mistake. They break up the continuity of pledge observance. They furnish one more preaching service, whereas one of the great advantages of the Christian Endeavor prayer meeting is that it is so essentially different from the other services of the day, if your meeting is held on Sunday, that it does not fatigue the participants. My own observations have been that such departures from the legitimate work of Christian Endeavor societies do more harm than good.

The Time for Meeting. — It is still undecided when is the best time to hold Christian Endeavor prayer meetings, — whether before or after the Sunday evening meeting of the church, or on some week-day evening. Probably the time never can be uniform, since the circumstances of the different churches vary so widely.

The majority of societies hold their meetings just before the evening service of the church, and in many churches the pastor ascends the pulpit immediately after the conclusion of the Christian Endeavor prayer meeting, so that the two services are really one, each being, of course, shorter than an hour.

Many wise pastors prefer, however, to have the Christian Endeavor service come after the evening preaching service, and to use it for an after-meeting. The older people like to remain, and those that are interested in the pastor's words stay to see what the same Christianity he has been preaching can do for younger people.

A Summarist. — It often happens that some of the most helpful things said in the course of a Christian Endeavor meeting are spoken at the beginning, but these are likely to be quite forgotten before the close of the evening. For the purpose of reviving these, and at the same time bringing the meeting to a focus, some societies have adopted the helpful custom of appointing a summarist, who occupies a minute or two just before the last hymn in reading a paper upon which he has written the most helpful thoughts expressed in the course of the evening.

This summarist is appointed by the president, and is a different person each week. Since all the members know that they are likely to be called upon in this capacity, they are more attentive at every meeting, that they may be able to accomplish the work well when it falls to their lot. Thus a double point is gained.

What Seven Did. — As a bit of inspiration to prayer-meeting committees that are laboring under difficulties and feel discouraged, it is well worth while to repeat here the account of one of the regular meetings of a California society of only seven members about which I have heard.

There was first a ten-minute praise service of prayer songs, prayer being the subject of the evening. Then came a moment of silent prayer, after which the members read in concert the sixty-first psalm. The prayer-meeting committee then led a Bible-reading, whose subject was, " The Bible teachings with regard to prayer." In answer to the leader's question, " What is prayer?" five members gave their answers. Then came quotations and poems taken from " Aids to Endeavor," and sentence prayers in which one prayed who had never prayed before. Following this, one member recited a poem, " Answered Prayer," and another told about the emphasis B. Fay Mills puts upon prayer in his meetings, and at the close were prayers for special objects.

If a meeting of so much interest and variety can be conducted by a society so small, can any of us find an excuse for poor meetings in our larger societies?

An Open Parliament. — Open parliaments may occupy occasionally a portion of the time of the Christian Endeavor prayer meeting. For example, such a topic as "Our duties in the Sunday morning services" might well be discussed by different members, especially when the topic has something to do with Sabbath observance.

The Benediction. — The Mizpah benediction has come in common use in our Christian Endeavor societies. It is the sentence found in Genesis 31 : 49, "The Lord watch between me and thee, when we are absent one from another." It is not always correctly given, and the exact wording should be noticed.

An occasional use is recommended of this sentence from the psalms: "Let the words of our mouths and the meditations of our hearts be acceptable in thy sight, O Lord, our Strength and our Redeemer." Also of this benediction from Numbers 6 : 24–26 :

> "The Lord bless thee and keep thee:
> The Lord make his face shine upon thee, and be gracious unto thee:
> The Lord lift up his countenance upon thee, and give thee peace."

The latter form of benediction is especially beautiful and appropriate.

A Rule Worth Remembering. — Some Endeavorers find difficulty in knowing just when they are speaking loudly enough and not too loud. The regular elocutionist's rule is worth remembering, — *Speak to the people that are farthest away from you* if you have those in mind, and those only, you will speak loudly enough for all to hear, and yet not so loudly as to be disagreeable.

Volunteers. — The chairman of the prayer-meeting committee may occasionally call for volunteers for the next meeting. The call may be, "Let those stand who will lead in prayer during the next meeting," or, "Let those rise who will have some words to say on the topic of the next meeting." In this way a certain part of the society is set to very definite thinking during the week.

Writing Comments. — The prayer-meeting committee should keep its eye on the members that are too diffident or too slothful to take part in the meeting except by reading a verse. An excellent plan is to make special requests that such members write out something regarding the topic, and hand it to the member of the committee who prefers the request. He will correct it, and then hand it back for reading in the meeting.

The Cold End of the Meeting. — The prayer-meeting committee must see to it that the opening of the meeting is provided with speakers ready to push things, but nevertheless it must look after the cold end of the meeting, — that time toward the close when the majority have spoken, and the meeting is likely to lag. For this period let some of the committee reserve their contributions, or have some plan to propose, — such as a series of sentence prayers, or the concert reading of a hymn, or a repetition in concert of some familiar passage of Scripture, or to call upon some visitor for a few words of counsel, — that may render the close of the meeting as hearty as its beginning. Take care of the ends of the meeting, and the middle will take care of itself.

Starters. — I have heard of a society a few of whose members conspired to form what they called a band of "first getters-up." That is capital.

Mr. Moody tells how he started a revival in a dying church. He got ten men to promise to be the *first* to take part at the next prayer meeting. These ten rose at the same time. Such a thing was never known in that church before, and the revival began at once.

It defies grammar, but let us have ten "firsts" in every church; and who so well fitted to watch this beginning of a meeting as the members of the prayer-meeting committee?

After the Close. — Much of the spiritual effect of our Christian Endeavor meetings is dissipated in the worldly chit-chat and gossip into which the prayer-meeting attendants are likely to fall during the interval between the close of the prayer meeting and the beginning of the evening service. Conscientious members of the prayer-meeting committee may effect a reform if they will distribute themselves throughout the room, and earnestly strive to keep the after-meeting conversation blessedly in line with the theme of the meeting. Why is it that we are so hesitant to talk with one another about religious truths, anyway?

For Answer in the Meeting. — Every week the

prayer-meeting pages of some Christian Endeavor papers give a series of questions bearing upon the Christian Endeavor topic of the week. If you have no such paper, make up your own questions. These questions are intended to stimulate thought, and to lead to the giving of personal testimony instead of the mere reading of a verse of Scripture. Many prayer-meeting committees have adopted the excellent plan of cutting out these questions, pasting them on separate slips of paper, and handing these slips at the previous meeting to members whom it is desired to get out of the verse-reading class.

Another way is to hand out these slips at the meeting when the topic is to be discussed, or to write the questions upon a blackboard, placing it before the society, and asking the members to answer any questions they choose. Sometimes it is well to assign one question to several Endeavorers, that their answers may be compared. Sometimes the leader will read the questions in order, calling upon previously designated members to give their answers. At other times these answers will come in the course of the meeting, with no reference to the previous giving out of the questions. Sometimes the prayer-meeting committee will prepare its own questions, and occasionally the members will themselves be requested to come prepared with questions on the topic which they will propound for the leader himself to answer, or, if the leader cannot answer them, the pastor or some older Endeavorer may be requested to do so.

A Useful Pause. — Place upon the blackboard the questions just described. About the middle of the meeting announce that a full five minutes will be devoted to silent communion and meditation upon the thoughts presented upon the blackboard. During these five minutes there must be no speaking, singing, or audible prayer. This exercise will add much to the impressiveness of the meeting, and to the value of the latter portion of it, besides teaching the members how to prepare for succeeding meetings.

Use of the Blackboard. — No Christian Endeavor society is well equipped for its work that does not possess a blackboard, or some substitute for it. A portable blackboard is easily made, or may be bought cheaply. Wood, cloth, or slate are the best materials. If for any reason a blackboard is not be obtained, you can at least use large sheets of manilla paper, with some dark-colored chalk.

The uses of a blackboard are almost infinite, and increase as a society becomes accustomed to it. A set of questions upon the topic, written on the blackboard, will suggest testimonies and little talks from the members, and will be a strong stimulus to many a meeting.

It is well for the leader to write upon the blackboard the divisions of the topic as he wishes it considered. In a conspicuous part of the blackboard may be printed the subject of the meeting, with the place where the Scripture passage is found, and possibly the numbers of the hymns to be used. Any notice it is desirable to bring before the society conspicuously may be written upon the board. Many leaders are skilled in the use of diagrams, and important truths can be fixed in this way upon the memory.

One of the best ways of conducting a consecration meeting is to write the names of members upon the board, asking them to take part in that order, the secretary noting the participation without calling the names. Upon the board may be written passages of Scripture to be read by the society in concert.

Many if not all of our Christian Endeavor topics could be attractively illustrated on the blackboard, and if your society has any one skilled in the use of chalk, he should be utilized in this way. Very often the blackboard illustrations for the Junior topic given in the Christian Endeavor papers would be suitable also for the topic of the older society, and the ingenuity of the artist will supply others. If the picture is placed before the society it will do its work in silence and need not be referred to, though a good picture is almost certain to be referred to by some one in the course of the evening.

The Front Seats. — I am not one of those that feel like urging, at all times, that the front seats be compactly filled. It does not annoy me when the audience sits in the back part of the room, and I am not afraid of the rows of empty benches between me and them. This is because I believe that the ideal arrangement, both for seeing and hearing, is a wide semi-circle, with the leader in the centre.

It can always be felt, however, when the empty

front seats are causing a coldness and stiffness; and when the prayer-meeting committee sees this to be the case, effort should be made to close up the ranks. In my own society, at one time, there was a bold call for volunteers who would promise always to sit in the row of seats next the front, or, if those seats were occupied, as far forward as might be. Nearly every one in the room promptly rose to signify his promise to do this, and we had no more trouble with front seats. Such a "front seat brigade" might be formed in any society.

Possibly a better plan is the appointment of ushers, two of the younger lads, one for each door, or for each side of the room; and these will seat the members as far forward as is deemed necessary. It is better that ushers should be appointed, than that the social committee should do this work. The social committee should be free to meet the strangers, introduce them to the members, sit down by them, and make them feel at home throughout the evening.

One of the best preventives of this front seat difficulty is to have no more seats in the room than are likely to be needed. It is far better to bring in chairs to accommodate an unusually large crowd, than to have empty chairs staring the society in the face during the meeting.

You may turn the seats in the back rows entirely around, reversing the chairs only when they are needed after the front ones have been filled up. The ushers may stretch a cord along the aisle, shutting off these seats from occupation until the front ones are filled. The back seats may be tipped forward against those in front, signifying that they are reserved for the late comers. Or, the ushers may politely request those who have taken the back seats to move forward, telling them the reason why.

Another ingenious cure for the back seat habit is the following placard, posted conspicuously in the prayer-meeting room. No one who reads it will care to be found in a back seat if a front seat is obtainable:

IF YOU WANT A BACK SEAT AT THE
PRAYER MEETING
YOU WILL HAVE TO COME EARLY.

Some societies place in the vestibule of the prayer-meeting room, facing the entrance, a large board, bearing this staring inscription: "Please come to the front."

CHAPTER XII.

SPECIAL MEETINGS.

Their Value. — There is danger of having too many "special meetings"; there is greater danger of having too few. When a cart is jerked out of the rut, it is very likely to start for the other side of the road instead of keeping straight forward; but that is better than staying in the rut. We must have variety in our meetings; we must not make a hobby horse of this same variety.

There is virtue, however, in a new method, just because it is new. It may not be as good as the old way, but its freshness will waken your society and invigorate it more than the better old way could, and after trying the new you will go back to the old with new zest and appreciation. Therefore I beseech all readers of this book to use this chapter, but to use it wisely. When you see that the meetings have begun to drag and that they need some stimulus of novelty, then, and not till then, put in practice some one of the following suggestions; and when the new plan has done its work, give it up, and return to the good old ways.

Memory Meetings. — One of the best modes of getting out of the ruts, is a memory meeting. Everything at this meeting is based upon the memory.

There are to be no books, with the single exception of a hymn-book granted the organist. The leader must commit to memory the Scripture reference for the evening, and everything he proposes to say. All verses must be repeated, hymns must be called for without consulting the hymn-books, and by name if the numbers are not familiarly known, and every one must sing from memory. It would be well to make one of the exercises of the evening a repetition of the pledge from memory, and there should be also the concert repetition, in the same way, of familiar passages of Scripture, as well as of familiar hymns.

A Sample Memory Meeting. — Not all our Endeavorers, though an increasing number of them, appreciate the usefulness of memory meetings. I have been very much interested in a pleasant account of a memory meeting that appeared in *North and West.* May the reading of it prompt many societies to hold prayer meetings of this useful form:

Suppose all the hymn-books were stolen away and all the Bibles were burned up, as in the days of persecutions! Suppose we were blind, and could not use our helps in worship as we do. Perhaps the lights fail us. Perhaps we are at a summer resort where all the devotional aids are missing, as is apt to be the case. Shall we therefore have no services? That is a very frequent result. But it is not the best way to spend a sacred day.

The fathers used to have vesper praise service at home every Sabbath evening. In the days when books were scarcer, and when the hymns were fewer in number, when the hymns were lined out a verse at a time, and worshippers had to depend upon their memory rather than their eyesight, people learned more hymns than they do now. It was easy to sit in the gloaming of a holy day and swing these censers of song whose incense went up from the home altar of the manse to the celestial courts. Precious stanzas of praise had been hidden in our hearts, and every tender, holy sentiment could find voice in rhythmic verse.

So when our pastor did not preach those August evenings, our elders and Endeavor society held a memory meeting in which no written or printed helps were to be spread before the eye. The hour opened with "Jesus, Lover of my Soul." Then all repeated the Lord's Prayer. Another well known hymn, and all rose to repeat the Apostles' Creed. Then the Ten Commandments came, with some hesitancy on the second and fourth, which were the long ones. The minister got one of the short ones out of place, too. In some of the gospel songs it was odd to note how much stronger and firmer the chorus was than other portions, especially after the first verse. People rarely master the thought. The lines go into the eye word by word and out again, leaving an impression and nothing more.

The lesson topic was from the first chapter of John, and the leader had committed the classic introduction which begins that gospel. His attention had been so directed to the emphatic words, and to the reason for using certain verbs and expressions, that he brought out its meaning far better than if he had read it hastily without real study, or had skimmed some comment about it. A number of people had passages of precious promise and comfort. A daughter led us all in giving the twenty-third psalm.

As a help in prayer, Calvin had his confession, which ne had all the congregation join in repeating. This came in appropriately here. "Almighty and most merciful Father, we have erred and strayed from thy ways like lost sheep. We have followed too much the devices and desires of our own hearts. We have offended against thy holy laws. We have left undone those things which we ought to have done, and we have done those things which we ought not to have done, and there is no health in us. But thou, O Lord, have mercy upon us, miserable offenders. Spare thou those, O God, who confess their faults. Restore thou those who are penitent; according to thy promises declared unto mankind in Christ Jesus our Lord. And grant, O most merciful Father, for his sake, that we may hereafter live a godly, righteous, and sober life, to the glory of thy holy name. Amen."

A Scotch brother recalled an old hymn as sweet as a heathered hill, and one that is doubtless out of print. His prayer must be in large part a reminiscence of Dr. Guthrie's, for he sat under that illustrious divine until he learned the language of Canaan.

But many, alas, could remember nothing. One tried the *Gloria in Excelsis*. No one attempted the *Te Deum Laudamus*. Not a single chapter from the Bible could be quoted even in partial completeness. Most were rusty even in the catechism. It was a delightful meeting, but it emphasized the importance of cultivating the memory. Much of our worship is too vague. It would be well to master and remember more devotional material.

The Consecration Meeting. — For a discussion of this most important topic I must refer the readers of this book to a pamphlet entitled, "The Crowning Meeting," published by the United Society of Christian Endeavor. Price ten cents. In that pamphlet, I have given a very large number of different ways of conducting a consecration meeting, to avoid formality, and yet get at the results that all consecration meetings should seek. Here are a few methods for varying the consecration meetings that have been brought to my attention since writing that pamphlet.

Instruct the secretary to make a separate list of those members whom he knows to be absent, and read this list after the rest. A slight glance over the audience will often show him just who are absent, so that he can add to his list even after he reaches the prayer-meeting room. This plan gives unity to the meeting, and avoids the pause that sometimes occurs after the reading of an absent member's name.

In some large societies it may be well to appoint a special consecration committee to care for the interests of the consecration meeting. There are many things that such a committee could do. It could suggest to the members that are in the habit of merely reading a verse, other ways of participating. It could plan fresh ways of conducting the meeting. It could make it its business to keep the consecration meeting prominently before the members during the month. It could get more experience-telling into meetings. Best of all, it could make its own members models of the right way to take part in a consecration meeting, — prayerfully, humbly, earnestly.

Other Methods. — It will be of use to give here a brief statement of some of the methods of varying the consecration meeting that are described fully, with others, in the pamphlet above referred to.

The secretary may call the letters of the alphabet, pausing after each letter for the members whose names begin with that letter to take part in any order they choose. The members present may be divided into sections, those in different blocks of seats taking part in order, as their section is called. You may occasionally hold a voluntary consecration meeting, the members taking part promptly in their own order, the secretary calling at the close the list of the members that have not taken part.

There may be a prayer consecration meeting, in which each member may participate by offering prayer. The roll, in this case, should not be called. In a committee consecration meeting the roll is called by committees. These rise and take part, the chairman leading, in some way appropriate to their committee work.

At a " next step " consecration meeting the Endeavorers are invited to take part, each one of them, in the way he finds most difficult. At the consecration meeting next after the election of officers, these officers and the new committees may take part with special reference to the new work they have undertaken.

At a " C. E." consecration meeting the question, " What does Christian Endeavor mean to you? " is the basis of the evening's thought, and each member brings two verses to answer the question, one beginning with the letter C and the other with the letter E, illustrating them with personal comments. At a song consecration meeting the members sing their consecration, or express it by reading passages from hymns.

At all these meetings, though the roll may not be called, the secretary should carefully note who takes part. When the roll is called, it should not uniformly be called in the same way. Sometimes begin with the end of the alphabet and call the roll backwards. Occasionally call three or four names at a time, the members responding in the order in which their names are called. Sometimes print a list of the members in large letters on the blackboard, or furnish each member with a list prepared on a hectograph, and have them give their testimony without any other roll-call. Where there is a pause, the secretary will read the name of the absent member, as a token that the next in order should take part.

The associate members' names, if called at all during the consecration meeting, should be called at the opening and from a separate list. The associates should not be expected to do more than answer " Present," though they should be permitted, of course, to do more, if they desire.

Every consecration meeting should open, and, possibly, close with the concert repetition of the pledge.

In the Order of Badges. — Some societies carry on the consecration meeting without a roll-call, in this way. On a rack at the entrance hang badges, each bearing a number. The members themselves have numbers to correspond, and as each member comes in he takes down his own number and wears the badge throughout the meeting. The members take part in the order of their numbers, without a roll-call. The secretary has before him the rack from which the badges have been removed, and can tell at once what numbers are not present. When the time for these numbers comes, he simply announces them, indicating that the members belonging to them are not present, and that the Endeavorer whose number comes next is to speak. At the close of the meeting the Endeavorers going out throw their badges into a receptacle, and this makes material for the records of the secretary and the lookout committee.

Letter Evening. — Preparation for this meeting must be begun long before. The prayer-meeting committee will write to Endeavorers in different parts of the country, preferably to the old members of the society that have left town, and to former members of the church that have removed their residence, or to ministers and distinguished Christians that are personally known to the members of the society. All these will be informed regarding the plan of the meeting, and asked to send some message upon the topic of that night.

The reading of these messages will occupy nearly all the time of the evening, and will prove a pleasant link joining the old members to the present work of the society. Applications for messages should not be made, of course, to persons that have no personal interest in the society.

Suggestion Meetings. — An occasional suggestion meeting will prove very helpful. Let each member write to some friend who is active in Christian Endeavor work, and ask him for a plan or a method which he thinks novel and helpful. On the appointed evening the letters received in response are read, and in this way there are focused upon one society the experiences of many widely scattered Endeavorers.

Post Office Days. — On Christian Endeavor post office day, the active members hand in letters that they have written to the Juniors and to the associate members. The letters are not written to special persons, but are handed in to the president, who, with the aid of the other officers, addresses them at the close of the Christian Endeavor service, and hands them to the Junior superintendent to be distributed to the Juniors.

Here is a sample letter once sent by an active to an associate member in distant Australia:

July 13, 1894.

Dear Friend: Why are you not an active member? We are glad to have you as an associate, but you mean to be an active member some day, do you not? Then why will you not be one now? If you do not love Jesus, then *now* is the very time to begin. You do not know anything of the future; all you have is the very present. I think everybody wants to make the best of his or her life; then is it not the best to give that life, with all its hopes and plans, into God's hand? Perhaps you have done this, but think you cannot do anything for him. Have you ever thought of that verse — "Co-laborers together with God"? O, is not that a high privilege; do you not want to claim it? I pray that you may do so to-day. I think we all want to remember more that we are "trusting in the Lord Jesus for strength," and not in ourselves. If we remember this all the days of every week of every year, I think we should be different.

I remain yours sincerely,
ACTIVE MEMBER.

Sunrise Prayer Meetings. — It is to be hoped that the Christian Endeavor societies understand by this time the blessing that can be gained from an occasional sunrise prayer meeting. The slight exertion needed to get out at that early hour, the unusual time and surroundings, the feeling of enterprise, all combine to give zest to these meetings; while the fact that the members are at the very beginning of the day contributes to the thoughtfulness of the exercises.

The most fitting times for sunrise prayer meetings are Christmas, New Year's day, and Easter. These early morning prayer meetings are now held in connection with the large Christian Endeavor conventions, and it would be a good idea for all societies to hold them at the time of the sessions of the International Convention, whose early morning prayer meetings are always the most spiritual and helpful of its meetings.

One of the most earnest of the society members, or the pastor of the church, should conduct the sunrise prayer meeting. A bright song service should be held while the late ones are arriving, and there should be much prayer throughout the hour. A good deal of care should be taken in selecting the theme, which should always be bright, cheery, and forward-looking. No thought is more suitable than that of consecration, — consecration to the highest ideals; consecration to the work God has set before us in the day or year to come.

The older members of the church will always like to join in these early morning prayer meetings, and an earnest invitation to do so should always be given them.

Morning by Morning. — Where the spiritual tide of the society has begun to run low, a succession of morning prayer meetings will sometimes be found just what the society needs. Not all the members may come, but you will find that those that do come will receive an impetus for the day's service that will uplift even those that remain in their beds.

Some societies have adopted the plan of transferring to the early morning the regular society prayer meeting, thus relieving the evening programme of the church, and affording the young people a magnificent opening of the day's worship.

A Moonlight Prayer Meeting. — The same good results that attend sunrise prayer meetings might be expected to attend those held by moonlight. The strangeness of the surroundings gets the society out of the ruts, and the beauty and solemnity of the scene is always impressive. Such meetings held occasionally, of course in the warmer months, when alone out door meetings are possible, serve very pleasantly to break up the monotony of the ordinary work.

A Sealed Order Meeting. — This meeting carries out the analogy of the sealed orders given to captains as they set out on their voyages, the orders to be opened after they have left the shore and gone a certain distance. Before the beginning of the meeting the prayer-meeting committee passes around little slips, each containing directions for participation in the meeting. Of course the plan must be mentioned at the preceding meeting, and the co-operation of the Endeavorers gained at that time. The slips will request one Endeavorer to offer prayer, another to give a comment on a certain Bible verse, another to read certain stanzas of some hymn, and so on. Of course the requests will be fitted to the capabilities of each recipient.

A Biographical Meeting. — Practically all of our Christian Endeavor topics can be illustrated copiously by the lives of well-known men and women. Once in a while the prayer-meeting committee may wish to conduct a biographical meeting. Careful preparations should be made some time beforehand. The lives of the chosen heroes and heroines should be obtained from the public library or from private sources, and distributed to suitable persons, who will prepare themselves to speak at length or briefly, as the committee may direct, or, possibly, to read some short paper, or some extract from the book. This portion of the evening's exercises should not occupy more than fifteen or twenty minutes, and at the close every Endeavorer present should be given an opportunity to testify.

A Young Men's Meeting. — I have heard of a society that contained ten young men who had not led in public prayer and who determined to overcome their difficulties. They organized a prayer meeting which met twenty minutes before the regular prayer meeting, and in that meeting for young men alone they gained a confidence for the more public service. If the young men will take the lead in such matters, it will not be difficult for them to obtain a good following.

A Young Women's Meeting. — An evening entirely, or almost entirely, given up to the use of the young women of the society, may occasionally be helpful. The meeting is to be led by a young woman, and all that take a prominent part are to be of the same sex. The young men, however, are to be given an opportunity to keep their pledge with sentence prayers or very brief participation. This may be followed, of course, by a young men's meeting.

A Question Meeting. — Announce the plan of this meeting one week beforehand. Request the members to give careful study to the topic of the evening in connection with the Bible references, and to come each with two or three questions on the topic written on slips of paper. These questions are to be gathered and then distributed at random, so as to give each person present one or more. The meeting will consist of answers to these questions.

Question-Box Meetings. — The Uniform Topics always prescribe one question-box meeting in the course of the year, but these meetings are so helpful that many societies will wish to hold them oftener, or, if not to give up an entire evening to them, to open question-boxes during a portion of certain evenings. The feature should be announced distinctly one week beforehand. The Endeavorers must be asked to write out for the coming meeting clear and pointed questions, not merely on Christian Endeavor problems, but on any difficulty connected with the religious life.

Members of Christian Endeavor committees will ask for the solution of some of their difficulties. The officers of the society will ask questions tending to enforce some neglected principles. The pastor will find an opportunity to bring before the society some points he could not well bring out in other ways. Doubters will have an opportunity for the relief of their doubts. Students can bring in their Bible questions, and those whose friends are battling with any trouble may, by means of skillful questions, obtain for them some assistance.

The leader of this meeting should be the brightest and readiest member of the society. He should be quick to see a point and shrewd in expressing himself, and at the same time possessed of a good measure of tact. He should not, however, expect to answer even the majority of the questions himself. It will greatly help the meeting if he asks a large number of wise men and women of the church, including, of course, the pastor and the church officers, to attend that special Christian Endeavor meeting, for the purpose of answering questions that may be referred to them. The Sunday-school superintendent should of course be there, since many questions will refer to Sunday-school work. Besides, the leader should inform the society that he will call upon all members of the society, at his pleasure, to give what light they can upon any question.

After the opening exercises, ushers will collect the questions, which the leader will read without previously examining them. The questions should be read in a clear voice, so that all can understand them. It will be well for the leader, at the outset of the meeting, to urge extreme brevity upon all who may be called upon to answer. This brevity he will himself illustrate in his own replies to the questions.

In initiating this plan in your society, it will be well for the leader to arm himself beforehand with a number of questions, to be used in case the queries sent in by the members are not sufficiently numerous. If the meeting, however, is well talked up, there will be no fear of this. Hymns should be interspersed among the questions, and the meeting should not close without a few words of earnest prayer for

God's blessing upon it. I count this kind of meeting one of the most helpful in which a Christian Endeavor society can engage, and earnestly urge that it be held by every society at least once a year.

An Answer-Box. — Answer-boxes are not so commonly a feature of Christian Endeavor meetings as question-boxes, but they are almost equally valuable. The basis of an answer-box is a single question, propounded to the society one week beforehand. Answers to this question are to be written by the Endeavorers, and it would be well to state a limit of length. At the opening of the answer-box meeting these answers are collected, and are read by the leader. If it is thought best, the leader may comment upon the answers as he reads them, or may call upon some other Endeavorer to say a fitting word now and then. Prayers may also be interspersed, and appropriate songs.

Sometimes, instead of an answer-box, there may be held what may be called an answer meeting, previous warning having been given. This is like the meeting just described, with the exception that the answers to the question of the evening are not written beforehand, but are spoken by the Endeavorers, one after the other. This form of meeting is the more lively of the two. Such a question as, " Why do you belong to the Christian Endeavor Society?" would make a good topic for the answer-box; or such a topic as, " What is the greatest blessing you have found in the Christian life?" or, " What especial hindrance have you met with in your committee work?" or, "What method of Bible study have you found most helpful?" or, "How do you get your Sunday-school lesson?" or, "How can we interest strangers in this society and church?" or, "How can we help our pastor?" or, "What book, besides the Bible, has been most helpful to you in your Christian life?" Any question that deeply touches Christian experience or Christian work, makes a good basis for an answer meeting.

Associate Members' Meetings. — At least one evening in the year should be devoted to the needs of the associate members and to the unconverted. Of course by this I do not mean that these classes should not be constantly in mind. All our meetings should seek as their first end the salvation of souls; but during one meeting out of the fifty-two, if not oftener, *everything* in the meeting should tend toward this one aim.

For this meeting the lookout and the prayer-meeting committees should make special preparations. It should be led by the pastor, or, if he is prevented from doing this service, by some spiritually minded Endeavorer in your society. Every means should be used to obtain the attendance of the associate members and your unconverted friends. By previous conversations, get the more experienced workers to promise to give earnest personal testimonies, telling just what Christ has done for them, and how their membership in his church has been a blessing and a constant assistance.

Do not fail before the close of the meeting to call

for decisions for the Christian life. Simply the lifting of the hand will be sufficient, if it is clearly understood that this is in token that the person sincerely desires Christ's salvation from sin, and admission into his kingdom.

Post-Vacation Meetings. — One of the best meetings in the fall, after the Endeavorers have all returned from their summer outings, may be a post-vacation meeting. Every Endeavorer is to tell something connected with his summer experiences, — some lesson he has learned from his vacation, or some message of good cheer that he has to report from the summer.

A Star Meeting. — Programme committees for anniversaries and local celebrations, desirous of introducing brief talks on fundamental Christian Endeavor topics, may find this method helpful. Get some skillful-fingered worker to cut out of cardboard a large gilt star, to be suspended above the speaker's desk. Have a "C. E." monogram of silver paper, or, better yet, if feasible, of incandescent electric lights, placed in the centre, in order that it may be a C. E. star. On each of the five points of the star have inscribed one of the following topics: "The Pledge," "Relation to the Church," "Personal Consecration," "Committee Work," "The Junior Society." "The Pledge" could be placed on the point at the opening of the C. The subjects might then be treated consecutively by different members of the society. Perhaps it would be well to have the president show the unity of the whole in a two-minute talk at the close. His theme could be, "C. E. — Combined Excellences."

A Twentieth-Century Prayer Meeting. — It was a very novel way the young people of a certain society in Michigan once took to arouse the older members of the church to a sense of their responsibility to the weekly church prayer meeting. The story is interesting, moreover, as showing how, in one church, at least, the Endeavorers were more loyal to the church prayer meeting than the older church-members themselves.

In this especial church very few of the older members took any active part in the weekly prayer meeting, except a certain group, for whom every one else waited, no one outside of this group being even expected to take part. Nineteen of the young people decided that a change would be a good thing. They consulted with their pastor, and the following events were the result.

The pastor announced from his pulpit on Sunday that in place of the usual church prayer meeting they would hold a "twentieth-century prayer meeting," and he hoped that every one would be present. In the mean time the young people were dividing up the hour, arranging a programme which was known only among themselves. On the regular evening the room was well filled, many coming out of curiosity.

There was the ordinary opening service, and as soon as the pastor finished speaking an Endeavorer offered prayer, and then one after another spoke words of testimony, called for a hymn, or led in prayer, each taking part in accordance with the concerted programme. Not a pause occurred, not a moment was lost.

Just before the closing prayer, the pastor said he had been informed by the young people that the meeting was such a one as they intended to have in the twentieth century when they had become the older members of the church, but he hoped it would not be necessary to wait so long for another hour such as the one they had just spent. His hope has been fulfilled!

A Reporters' Evening. — For several weeks beforehand the members are to search out from Christian Endeavor papers interesting items regarding the work of other Christian Endeavor societies, helpful plans that may be incorporated into their own society, interesting items of denominational news. On the appointed evening there is to be a brief service on the regular topic, but the greater part of the evening is to be spent in listening to the different members as each brings one item that he has gleaned from this reading. The plan will probably set many to talking that have heretofore confined themselves to reading verses.

An Object Meeting. — An object meeting is especially valuable to the younger members and the associates. Every member is required to bring to the society some object, and to repeat some texts that the object illustrates, adding, if he is disposed, some comment of his own.

Convention Echo Meetings. — Whenever even one or two of the members of your society have attended a Christian Endeavor gathering, whether it be a local union convention, a State convention, or one of the great International Conventions, be sure to utilize, in the next practicable meeting, the enthusiasm the delegates have brought back with them. If only one or two have visited the convention, set apart ten or fifteen minutes for a report, previously notifying them that such a report is expected. But where more have been present, an entire evening may profitably be spent in reviewing the impressions made by the Christian Endeavor gathering.

The songs sung at the convention should be used. Extracts may be made from printed reports, but such extracts should be used very sparingly. The most helpful sayings should have been jotted down during the convention, to be reported at this echo meeting. Bits from the open parliaments and sunrise prayer meetings will be remembered. One of the most attractive parts of the echo meeting will be the review of the convention question-box, if the convention had such a feature, the questions being repeated, together with the answers given, so far as these can be remembered, and an opportunity being offered the Endeavorers to discuss these questions. At the close, some practised speaker should sum up his impressions of the convention, with whatever lessons it may have for the local society.

The decorations of the society room should repeat the convention colors, and the convention badge should be displayed. In every way the speakers should seek to make the members that were so unfortunate as to be obliged to remain at home, sharers with them in the pleasure and profit of the meetings they attended.

A Badge Service. — To carry on this meeting, ask the members, one week beforehand, to come to the next meeting prepared to give an interpretation of the Christian Endeavor initials, " C. E.," and to comment upon the interpretation given. For example, some may think that " C. E." means " Christian Every day," or " Christian Earnestness," or " Christ my Example." In the same way, the fuller initials, Y. P. S. C. E., may serve for the basis of a very helpful and interesting meeting.

Promise Meetings. — It is rare indeed that a year's Christian Endeavor topics do not contain at least one promise meeting. The most obvious mode of taking part in such a meeting is to repeat the promises of Scripture, each Endeavorer adding his personal comment, born of his own experience. It is helpful at such meetings for the leader to classify the promises, calling upon the members first, for example, to repeat Bible promises of strength, then of guidance, life, heaven, etc.

The prayer-meeting committee should collect beautiful poems regarding Bible promises, and give them out to the Endeavorers in time for them to commit them to memory, to repeat at the meeting. A certain section of the hour may be given to Christ's promises; another to the promises made to the patriarchs, the promises recorded in the psalms, or in the writings of Paul.

Many of these Bible promises have attaching to them interesting histories; they have helped great men and women at critical points in their lives; and these facts should form part of the substance of the promise meeting.

An interesting feature of such a meeting would be written answers to the question, "What promise has helped you most at critical periods of your life?" The members should be asked to write out answers to this question, and hand them in without signing their names, in order that their disclosure of soul experiences may be more frank.

An interesting song service may easily be based upon the Scripture promises, and members may be asked to join in sentence prayers, setting before them the model, "Father, I thank thee that thou hast said — " or, " Help me to accept thy promise that — ."

A Programme Meeting. — I do not believe that Christian Endeavor prayer meetings should uniformly be run in accordance with a programme, but I do believe that an occasional programme meeting is a great help and stimulus. Some societies have a special programme committee for the purpose of preparing these occasional meetings, but I should think it better to assign that work to the prayer-meeting committee.

The programme should, of course, have close reference to the topic of the evening. Temperance and missionary meetings submit themselves most easily to this style of treatment, but any of the regular topics may be used. Of course the consecration meeting should never be a programme meeting. Appropriate recitations, solos, duets, and quartettes, instrumental music of various kinds, addresses by the pastor and church officers, as well as by representative Endeavorers, and possibly by delegates from outside societies, — these are features suitable for the programme.

An Automatic Meeting. — This meeting is to have no leader. When the time for opening comes, some one will call for a hymn. On the conclusion of that, some one else, possibly, will call for another, or, better, start it with no announcement at all. There may be a call for sentence prayers, and, on the conclusion of these, an Endeavorer, without waiting for prompting, will speak briefly on the subject of the evening. Everything must be spontaneous, for a successful evening. It is best that absolutely no assignments be made, though of course, if there should be a hitch, the prayer-meeting committee will be ready to push things.

Of course the plan of the meeting must be carefully explained at the meeting of the week before. If your society is not in the habit of depending upon the leader for its inspiration, this plan will prove a delightful one for a change. If it is in the habit of depending on its leader too much, this plan is precisely the thing for the society to try.

When a society discovers how easy it is to have a good meeting without a leader, and how comparatively unimportant is the office of leader when the society does its part well, younger members may be more willing to take up the work of leading the meeting ; and all the members will feel more their responsibility for doing their best to make a meeting a success, whether a good leader is in the chair or an inexperienced one.

An Informal Prayer Meeting. — Sometimes the Christian Endeavor society can get itself out of the ruts by holding what is definitely known as an *informal* prayer meeting. Break up the ordinary arrangement of chairs by placing them in semicircles. The prayer-meeting committee may sit at a table in the midst of the congregation, and all of them should take part informally. Make the meeting, so far as possible, a conversation meeting, with many brief prayers, and with the impromptu starting of hymns.

A Comment Meeting. — In order to win members from the verse-readers' class, hold an occasional comment meeting. By vote of the society on the preceding week, obtain the promise of all the members that they will bring to this meeting verses of Scripture bearing upon the topic, each giving his own commentary on the same. These comments should be carefully prepared beforehand.

A State Meeting. — This form of prayer meeting is valuable only for large societies, and may be used for a consecration meeting. Instead of calling the names of the members the secretary will call their native States, and as each State or country is mentioned the members born there will rise and take part as the leader designates. A meeting of this sort is almost certain to be characterized by the telling of personal experiences.

An Evening for Beginners. — Select some evening with a topic on which much can be said by those that are inexperienced in prayer-meeting work, and make a special effort to bring out in new ways the ability of all your members. If you can, take a rising vote at the preceding meeting and see how many are willing to undertake at the next meeting, just for once, whatever line of work the prayer-meeting committee may set before them, — a word of prayer, or a brief testimony, — even though they have never attempted such a thing before. An earnest appeal for such a promise will scarcely fail to produce favorable results.

Have a beginner lead the meeting, — or two beginners, for dual leadership will be best. Make it understood that this is a beginners' meeting, and require even the older members to participate in the meeting, if possible, in some manner they have never attempted before.

A Rally Day. — Most societies feel the summer depression, either on account of the heat or on account of the absence of members on vacation; and most societies need some sort of rallying in the fall. It is better to make this a conspicuous feature of the society, and to open up a fall campaign strongly, than to trust to slow and spasmodic recovery from the summer languor. Here is a rallying summons that may be sent out by the prayer-meeting committee to all the members of the society:

Dear Friend: Summer is over, and the time for active, aggressive work is at hand. If we would gather in the rich harvest, each one must do his or her part. Every one can help and be helped by regular and prompt attendance at our meetings.

Next Sunday evening, September 1, at 7.15 o'clock, will be held the Rally Service of our society. We expect to see you present. God has richly blessed us in the past. May the future bring from his hands a more abundant blessing, and to this end may we always

>**R**ejoice in the Lord,
>**A**nd put your whole trust in him,
>**L**et us praise him continually.
>**L**aboring together with God,
>**Y**ou can do all things.
>
>**D**o good unto all men,
>**A**s you have opportunity.
>**Y**ield yourselves to God.
>
>**S**earch the Scriptures;
>**E**ndure all things;
>**P**ray without ceasing;
>**T**alk ye of all His wondrous works.
>1, 1895.

Please show your interest by being present. The subject of the meeting will be, "Enthusiasm, and what it will accomplish."

Sincerely yours in Christ,
Prayer-Meeting Committee.

At the meeting for that night the leader should be one of the most experienced of the society workers, and the thought of the meeting should look especially to the future, plans for the next year being proposed and discussed. Vacation experiences would, however, be also in order, and it would be profitable to devote a portion of the time of the evening to them. The main purpose, however, of the meeting is to give and get inspiration for the coming year's work.

A Model Meeting. — Prayer-meeting committees have a duty they owe to committees of other societies less favored, possibly, than they. I have heard of a society — one of the most fortunate in its State in regard to the number of earnest workers and the success with which their methods have been carried out — that decided to hold an ideal young people's prayer meeting, to which they invited delegates from the surrounding towns. The meeting-place was crowded, the meeting was spiritual and spirited, and those that were present thought it equal to a small convention.

A Call Meeting. — If the members of your society are on the whole earnest workers in the prayer meeting, you may venture upon a meeting planned after the following fashion. For the opening exercises the leader will call upon some Endeavorer to take part in a prescribed fashion, — praying, testifying, or reading a Bible verse. When this member has complied with the request, in his turn he has the privilege of calling upon some one else, and he upon a third, and so on, thus forming a chain of prayer-meeting participation that lasts through the evening.

A Motto Meeting. — Each member is to bring to the meeting a motto. These mottoes may be written and read, but it will be better if they are committed to memory. A word of comment should be added to each. To such meetings as these absent members should be asked to send contributions, as well as those present in town but not able to attend.

A Week of Meetings. — For a revival of interest in committee work, some societies have held a week of meetings under the direction of their different committees. One evening was prayer-meeting committee night; on another evening the society discussed their duties and responsibility with relation to the weekly prayer meeting; others were social committee night, missionary committee night, lookout committee night. All of these aroused the society in the direction of definite lines of work.

Besides, there might be a night for the associate members, a night for the Juniors, and so on. The exercises each evening will consist of one or more addresses, an open parliament, and much prayer. Why could not every society find inspiration in such a week of meetings?

CHAPTER XIII.

THE TOPIC CARDS.

Use the Uniform Topics. — There are very few societies now, though there were a large number at the beginning of the movement, that do not appreciate the great advantage of using the Uniform Topics prepared by the United Society of Christian Endeavor. These are sent out after a careful examination by a committee of representative pastors from the prominent evangelical denominations. They are chosen with careful regard to the precise needs of the Christian Endeavor societies. They have been used by millions of Endeavorers, and have been greatly blessed in the using. The societies that use them have open before them a very large number of commentaries, prepared by the wisest Christian scholars and most consecrated pastors. In visiting other societies one is sure what the topic will be; and besides, there is a stimulus in the thought that all over the world the minds of the Endeavorers are turned to the same subject.

The Special Meetings. — It is to be hoped that the Christian Endeavor societies will think twice before they omit from their topic cards any of the suggestions for special meetings made in the Uniform Topic cards. In these topics, for example, one meeting in the year whose theme is most fitting is indicated as a question-box meeting, another as a memory meeting, and on other dates are such special meetings as: a meeting for the associate members; one to be held in common with the Junior society; a meeting led by the pastor, and to consider the relations of the society and the church; a topical song service; a meeting for prayer alone; a meeting to consider the work of each committee; a patriotic service; a meeting regarding the work of the Sunday school; a Christian Endeavor Day meeting, and similar special meetings. All these are in addition to the four temperance and four missionary meetings, and the meetings on the regular holidays, Easter, Thanksgiving, Christmas, New Year's.

It should be remembered that the Uniform Topics are chosen with the greatest care. The union meeting with the Juniors, for example, — something so admirable in every society that has a younger society connected with it, — is placed at the time of the year and in connection with the topic that is most appropriate; and the society that wishes to get into its work as great a variety as possible will find that it can do this, usually, most easily and with least confusion by following strictly the order laid down in the Uniform Topics.

None of our societies I have so far observed are in danger of undertaking too many new methods. If they are in any danger, it is peril of the ruts. These special meetings give an excellent opportunity to inaugurate fresh plans, and to gain fresh enthusiasm.

The Society History. — A pleasant addition to any topic card will be a condensed history of the society; for instance, the date of its organization, the date of its adoption of important methods of work, the list of the past presidents of the society, and a summary of its prominent achievements.

Fans. — One wise society I have heard of printed the topics for the summer months upon two hundred fans that it distributed to the members. Thus at church and at home the topics were always kept before the eyes of the Endeavorers. This is a good plan for having a warm prayer meeting and keeping cool at the same time.

A Cross. — I have seen a very pretty topic card, on one page of which was printed the Christian Endeavor pledge, the words being arranged in the form of a cross, and above it the sentence, " When thou vowest a vow unto the Lord, neglect not to pay it." By the way, all our societies should know that the United Society has facilities for printing all kinds of topic cards, in the handsomest way, and at the lowest prices. All the profits of this work go to spread still further the blessings of the Christian Endeavor Society.

Their Duties. — I have heard of one society that prints on its topic card, under the names of the members that constitute each of its committees, a brief account of the most important work that committee is supposed to accomplish. The idea is an excellent one, as it keeps the duties of the various committees constantly before the eyes of the members.

A Swarm of Bees. — Prayer-meeting committees will do well to add to their topic cards brisk and brief suggestions regarding the conduct of the meetings. Here is a set of prayer-meeting Be's that may be hived on your topic card:

>Be prompt.
>Be prayerful.
>Be sincere.
>Be reverent.
>Be friendly with strangers.
>Be helpful to friends.
>Be consistent everywhere.
>Be Christlike always.

Another helpful set of suggestions is the following:

Be early.
Be joyous.
Do not apologize.
Do not try to be brilliant.
Do not pray or speak for over two minutes.
Do not be satisfied until souls are won to Christ.
Put your whole soul into everything you do.

Interlined Topic Cards. — Anything that will add to the usefulness and attractiveness of the topic card is a genuine aid in the society work. Sometimes, if the calendar for the year is printed upon the card, greater care will be taken of it, and it will be referred to more frequently. It is a good plan to print after each topic a very brief quotation appropriate to the subject.

Topic Memoranda. — Have you tried the plan of binding up with your topic cards or your " daily readings" seven or eight blank pages? You will thus convert your list of topics into a convenient book of memoranda, in which can be jotted down many helpful thoughts from the meetings.

The Last Page. — On the last page of the topic card should be placed something of general interest, helpful in the conduct of the meetings, as, for example, the following:

As an ACTIVE MEMBER
   "*Created in Christ Jesus unto good works.*" *Eph. 2 : 10.*
I promise
   "*My covenant will I not break, nor alter the thing that is gone out of my lips.*" *Ps. 89 : 34.*
to be true to all my duties
   "*Ye are my friends if ye do whatsoever I command you.*" *John 15 : 14.*
to be present at
   "*Then said the King . . . Be thou here present.*" *2 Sam. 20 : 4.*
and to take some part aside from singing
   "*Then they that feared the Lord spake often one to another.*" *Mal. 3 : 16.*
in every meeting
   "*Not forsaking the assembling of ourselves together, as the manner of some is.*" *Heb. 10 : 25.*
unless hindered by some reason which I can conscientiously give to my Lord and Master, Jesus Christ.
   "*Ye were also careful, but ye lacked opportunity.*" *Phil. 4 : 10.*

If obliged to be absent from the consecration meeting, I will, if possible, send an excuse for absence to the society.

"We, brethren, being taken from you for a short time, in presence, not in heart." 1 Thess. 2: 17.

Practical Points. — Here is a set of excellent suggestions that will be useful if incorporated in your topic card during some quarter:

Leaders of the meeting are limited in time to seven minutes, and may occupy the platform and conduct the meeting, or may arise in their accustomed places and open the subjects as they desire.

Under no circumstances must the meeting be more than an hour in length.

The surest way to make the meeting cold and unsatisfactory in every way, will be for the membership to seek out the remote corners of the room and maintain a gloomy silence.

Members and visitors are permitted to take part in the meeting in any way they see fit. "Where the spirit of the Lord is, there is liberty."

"GET TOGETHER," should be the motto of every meeting.

The singer who fails to sing is an abomination at the prayer meeting.

"What thou doest, do quickly," is a good motto for every one who takes part.

The Friday night meeting is *not* the "old folks'" meeting.

Come prepared for speaking. So shall thy words be as apples of gold in baskets of silver,

Leave your favorite hobby at home, and fit yourself into the subject and meeting.

Above all, come prayerfully. "Blessed are they that do hunger and thirst after righteousness, for they shall be filled."

A Prayer-Meeting Thermometer. — Here are two good ideas for the backs of topic cards:

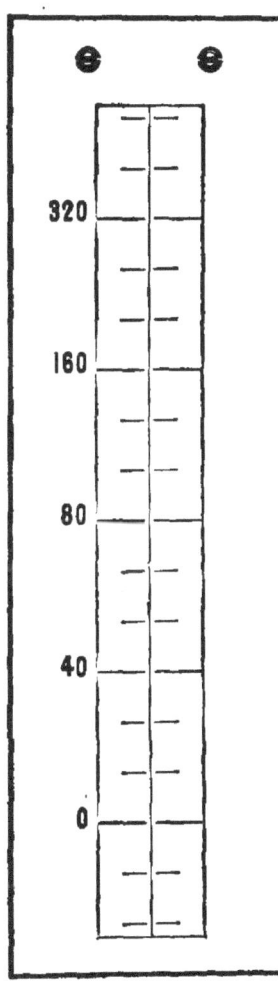

TAKE YOUR TEMPERATURE.

320 — Boiling. Enthusiastic, goes to meeting, gets others to go, works anywhere, in meeting or out of meeting.

160 — Blood heat. Very much alive, goes to meeting, leads the meeting, prays, speaks.

80 — Temperate. Alive, goes to meeting, takes part occasionally, usually found on a back seat.

40 — Freezing. Dying, goes to meeting occasionally, never takes part.

0 — Zero. Dead, never goes to meeting.

What is your temperature?

Read Rev. 3 : 15, 16.

OUR PLEDGE.

(a)
To Christ
Trusting in the Lord Jesus Christ for strength, I promise him that I will strive to do whatever he would like to have me do; that I will make it the rule of my life to pray and read the Bible every day,

(b)
To the Church
and to support my own church in every way, especially by attending all her regular Sunday and midweek services, unless prevented by some reason which I can conscientiously give to my Saviour, and that, just so far as I know how, throughout my whole life, I will endeavor to lead a Christian life.

(c)
To the Society
As an active member, I promise to be true to all my duties, to be present at and take some part, aside from singing, in every Christian Endeavor prayer meeting, unless hindered by some reason which I can conscientiously give to my Lord and Master. If obliged to be absent from the monthly consecration meeting of the society, I will, if possible, send at least a verse of Scripture to be read in response to my name at the roll-call.

Church Topics Also. — The Christian Endeavorers should make unselfish use of their topic card by announcing thereon, in addition to their meetings, those of the church, — the time and place, together with a hearty invitation to all young people to join in them.

CHAPTER XIV.

SOME CLOSING SUGGESTIONS.

To be a good prayer-meeting follower is as good as to be a good prayer-meeting leader. The best Endeavorer is both.

Do you know your Bible? Yes? Good! Now, then, do you know your hymn-book?

Prayer-meeting helps on the topic become prayer-meeting hindrances as soon as they cease to be suggestions and become "selections." A crutch is good for a cripple, but for a well man it's only a cause of stumbling. These helps should not be used as crutches, but as guide-posts.

Are you satisfied if only part of your meetings are good? Do you take it as a matter of course that a dull meeting should come now and then? Do you really believe that the Holy Spirit is changeable and fickle, and not able to give you glorious meetings all the time?

If you know how to follow a meeting, you'll have no trouble in leading it.

You may pass a hymn-book with an air that makes it an act of discourtesy, or you may convert the little kindness into a genuine invitation to Christ.

"Don't let precious moments pass unimproved," says an Endeavor paper. "As soon as the meeting commences to drag, close at once." Wouldn't it be better to inject a little life into it? You don't shoot a horse as soon as it begins to stumble.

A good topic card packed with information about the society will be almost as good as an added committee.

What the prayer meeting does for you is a good measure of what you are doing for it.

"A good prayer meeting is one led by anybody, partaken of by everybody, monopolized by nobody, and where everybody is somebody."

"Ambrose never heard of a Christian Endeavor meeting, but his counsel is pertinent, — 'If we must give account of every "idle word," take care, also, lest you have to answer for an idle silence.'"

"The one thing to make taking part easy is to study from Monday to Saturday."

SOME CLOSING SUGGESTIONS.

Endeavorer, when any one asks you what was your best prayer meeting, say, "My next."

If you can't pray short prayers, why, don't pray at all. These men who make long prayers are generally the ones that pray least at home. They are generally prayerless prayers, and they take the spirit right out of the meeting. — *D. L. Moody.*

"Be thoroughly prepared for the prayer meeting. Be brief. If prepared, you will be brief."

How to pray. A clergyman of Manchester, England, says that the Christian Endeavor solution of that problem is, if you want to learn to pray, pray, *pray.*

A Christian Endeavor topic card contains on the back this suggestive quotation: "Don't look around every time some one comes in. Study to be quiet. 1 Thess. 4: 11."

An Australian Endeavorer gives two excellent reasons for the prompt closing of Christian Endeavor meetings. "In the first place, because we promise in our pledge to be true to all our duties, and it sometimes happens that the home circle is deprived of its rights, and other important duties are neglected, by prolonged meetings. In the second place, some of the Endeavorers live at a distance, and it is neither kind nor wise to detain them."

Here is some good advice from Canada. It is pointed at all who have to speak at Christian Endeavor meetings. "Don't talk long, but speak clearly. Don't aim to tickle, but lead, impress. *Don't be afraid to stand up.*"

A certain Methodist Episcopal Endeavor society has this fivefold motto: "Prayer, Preparation, Punctuality, Participation, and Progress."

A writer tells about a Christian Endeavor society, advertised to begin at 6.30, in whose room he waited, as the members sauntered in, until, at 6.56, the leader opened the meeting. And what hymn do you think was announced? "Come to the Saviour, make no delay!"

A well-known Congregational minister of Australia became discouraged about his society, and one night he said, "Now we are going to pray, and God wants every active member to pray." They knelt down, and fifteen prayed right away, whose voices had never been heard before. That was the Pentecost of that society.

"The best way to get Christ to come to your prayer meetings, is to bring him with you."

"BREVITY!" This single word in large letters, visible from the very back seat, is emblazoned on a

SOME CLOSING SUGGESTIONS.

card that is posted in the meeting-room of a certain Presbyterian Christian Endeavor society. Duplicates might well be furnished to every society in the world.

A sensible Endeavorer urges that a well-known clause in the Christian Endeavor pledge be thus amended, — "To take some part in every meeting, *and to take that part distinctly.*"

The next time you hear the excuse, "I'm really too timid to speak in prayer meeting. If I only had the confidence of that Miss B——!" just ask the speaker if what she wishes for is not Miss B——'s eloquence and wisdom, and if her timidity would not disappear promptly if she felt that she could make a good show before men.

Translate *pausa* by the first personal pronoun. This is not Latin, but leadership.

"A new type of addresses is suggested, viz., *one-legged addresses*. It is said that Africans, when they "palaver," make one-legged speeches, *i. e.*, talk as long as they can stand on one leg. Not a bad suggestion for our Endeavor societies. Try it."

Here is a very suggestive reply given in a Minnesota convention to the question how to make prayer meetings interesting: "We try to find out in every meeting how the topic can help us in our every-day work and play."

Study variety in the service, — rather than have two meetings just alike, face the chairs the other way. — *Rev. F. E. Clark.*

Remember Plato's saying, "Good things are hard." Has a particular line of Christian work become easy for you? Then go on to something harder; not because it is harder; but because, for you and your little world, it is better.

As Christian soldiers, the prayer meeting should be to you the recruiting and supply station, the ammunition wagon with which to wage successfully a week's warfare against the world and the devil. Never make the fatal mistake of considering the prayer meeting a battle-ground. — *William T. Ellis.*

"A prayer meeting should never be *conducted*. It is not a machine to be run with belts and pulleys and *cranks*. Let it be voluntary, spontaneous."

The story is told of Mr. Spurgeon that one day a member of his congregation, who was in the habit of making long prayers, wore out the great preacher's patience with his endless petitions. Mr. Spurgeon quietly went up to him and said, "Brother, you've prayed long enough; and if you feel offended at my saying so, you will be a goose." That is the best way to deal with such people.

The leader has planned long for this meeting. He has prayed hard over it. He has selected every hymn with care. He has studied the best way to read the Bible verses, and he has chosen every word he shall say with nice regard to its possible effect. Right in the midst of this most thoughtfully prepared beginning, the door opens, and some one comes rustling in, walks with creaking boots up the long aisle, and takes his seat with a roguish grin, looking at his watch. All heads turn, and all hearts are turned from the topic. The opening is spoiled. Is this newcomer *you*?

"Prompt payment is sure payment. Delay is the fruitful source of failure. The Christian Endeavorer who waits for a more convenient moment to take part in the meeting usually fails to find it. The surest cure for hesitation is to take the first chance. Putting off a duty is putting away power to perform it."

Because Paul said "This one thing I do," many Christians think themselves wise in sticking to one mode of Christian work. A verse read at prayer meeting, a hymn started, a tract a week,— some such "one thing" contents them. Paul's "one thing" was as complex as the Columbian Exposition. It included oratory, quiet conversation, prayer, song, letter-writing, debate, voyages, organization, chains, mockings, rebukes, praises, — why, what did it not include? That is not a safe text for lazy folks to quote!

If the appointed leader be kept from coming, and you are asked to lead, and refuse, though you know yourself more capable without preparation than the prepared leader, — what honest name will you give that refusal?

You find it hard work to speak or pray in public? Show me a Christian who has always found it easy, and I will show you a man who deserves no credit for his speaking and praying in public, as he himself would be the first humbly to acknowledge. In war, that officer wins promotion who captures an obstinate garrison, not the officer who raises his flag over a deserted fort.

Four things constitute a good prayer-meeting leader: prayerfulness, patience, promptness, and point.

And now may the one aim and result of all our Christian Endeavor prayer meetings be the glory of God in the salvation of human souls!

CHAPTER XV.

A BUDGET OF FRESH METHODS

The following prayer-meeting plans, original with the author, so far as he knows, and now first published, are added to the new edition of this book. It is hoped that they will prove useful in a multitude of prayer meetings.

Prayer-Meeting Specialists.— There are certain elements that should be cultivated in every prayer meeting, if it is to be as helpful as it may be; these are prayer, testimony, and singing. If we add the work of the leader, we shall have a very good outline of the prayer meeting. It is well for the members of the prayer-meeting committee to divide these elements among them, each taking one and seeking to develop the society along that line. The music will be assigned to the music committee, if there is one, but the prayer-meeting "specialists" on music will co-operate with that committee. If there is no one on the committee that is competent to lead the society in some one of these elements, you may go outside the committee for a specialist. The prayer specialist will try to increase the number of prayers in the meeting and to persuade those to pray that have not yet prayed in public. He will give brief suggestions on the subject from time to time, and he may organize little meetings for prayer made up of beginners in this noble service. The testimony specialist will give out questions and topics and illustrations, and will urge original participation in every way he can devise. The specialist in leading will advise each leader as to his plan for the meeting and the general conduct of it. This definite and systematic division of the work cannot fail to be helpful.

A Prayer Meeting by Periods.— The leader will divide the meeting into periods, a song period, a prayer period, a question-and-answer period, a Bible-verse period, an experience-and-testimony period, a purpose period, a closing-prayer period, a closing-song period. He will previously ask several Endeavorers to take part in each of the periods, say three for each period. A list of the periods will be placed before the society, and the leader will announce the beginning of each according to a time schedule, which he will have before him, but which he will not place before the society.

A Prayer-Meeting Mentor.— It will serve a good purpose if the society occasionally chooses one of its members to act for a month as a mentor of the meetings. If the mentor is merely one of the average Endeavorers, not some one of special ability, all the better, provided he is faithful. Suggestions from him will be more likely to be heeded than those coming from some one so brilliant that the society thinks his ideas far above them. The mentor will take brief notes during the meeting of things to blame and things to praise, and will speak of these very concisely at the close of the meeting. He will note the general conduct of the members as well as their participation in the meeting. A particularly helpful mentor may be chosen again after an interval.

A Discussion Class.— One of the best possible aids for the beginner in prayer-meeting work would be a discussion class. This should be conducted by a member of the prayer-meeting committee of especial ability and considerable experience, or by some one of that ability whom the committee persuades to do the work. The boys should be formed into a class by themselves, and the girls at another time into a class, or you may have both classes at the same time under different leaders. In the discussion class the prayer-meeting topic for the next Sunday will be discussed. The leader will not make speeches, but by questions and comments and all manner of encouragement will seek to bring out the thoughts of the beginners, or, rather, to teach them how to think and how to express their thoughts. The prayer-meeting questions of *The Christian Endeavor World* will be of great service here. The leader will especially try to lead the beginners to think of the experiences in their own lives that illustrate the topic, thus preparing them really to testify in the meeting. The discussion class will begin and end with prayers by the Endeavorers, and so will be also a class in prayer.

A Post-Office Meeting.— The leader of this meeting will mail to every member of the society on the Monday before his meeting a note asking him to take part in the meeting by sending to the leader at once a written comment on the topic, or a question on it, or some quotation from the Bible or from a secular author bearing on the topic, followed by an original comment on the quotation. If any wish, they may write original prayers on the subject of the meeting. The members are told that in the meeting each will be given some one else's communication to read, or question to answer. All the contributions will be read without the names of the writers. The leader will interpose comments upon the various contributions as they are read. You will find that the post-office will help you to have a very live meeting, for which the members will have made more preparation than usual.

Prayer Checks.— Simply for the sake of training the beginners in the art of public prayer, and not at all for a permanent plan, why not try the following? Give out a number of cardboard checks, as many as there are members in the society. Write upon each of these some subject for prayer, such as the society, the officers, the committees, the leader of the meeting, the meetings, the work of the year, the church, the pastor, the Sunday-school, the new members of the society, the new members of the church, the Junior society, the associate members, our town, our State, our nation, the special need of the world, home missions, foreign missions, the missionaries, the native converts, the immigrants, the President, Congress, our State legislature, our town officers, the temperance reform, etc. The subjects of prayer are endless, and you will soon have enough checks. Give out these checks as the members enter, and explain that when sentence prayers are called for from a certain portion of the room, those in that section are expected to offer brief prayers, remembering the causes written upon the slips. Each will receive a different check each night. The plan has great variety and may be continued helpfully for several meetings. The checks are to be placed in a box as the members leave the room.

A Placard that Means Business.— If the prayer-meeting committee finds that the members are becoming lax regarding any portion of the pledge that refers to the meeting, that portion may be printed in big black letters on a large sheet of paper and hung in front of the society, where every one will see it all through the meeting. For instance, " I promise to take some part in every meeting," or just " Some part," or merely " In every meeting." In the same way the part referring to the consecration meeting may be emphasized.

Volunteer Quartettes.— The prayer-meeting committee (or the music committee, if you have one) may ask the members to form themselves into fours for the purpose of practising hymns to sing to the society. These fours may be of boys or of girls, or mixed quartettes. They may sing in parts or in unison, as they please. They may choose a hymn from the society song book or from any other book they prefer. They will tell the chairman when they are ready and he will notify them on what evening they are to sing. They will stand in front of the society while singing. This plan will, if it is entered upon heartily, discover to the society much musical talent it had not suspected, and will add to the meeting an element of surprise and delight. Of course if the volunteering lags it will be stimulated by private work.

W. T. U. C.— The famous initials, W. C. T. U., may be turned around and become W. T. U. C. Get a group of active young fellows who would enjoy such a secret to join the W. T. U. C., wearing at the meeting badges setting forth the mysterious initials. They mean "Wake Them Up Club," and all who join the club agree to help do something at every prayer meeting to wake it up and keep it out of the ruts. It will be something different every time, so that the members will be kept guessing what will come next. Sometimes the club will sit in the very front seats that were never known to be occupied before. Sometimes they will get up and sing an appropriate song. Sometimes they will take part in swift succession one after the other, and all of them with original testimony. Sometimes they will start a hymn without the piano. Sometimes they will repeat a fine Bible passage suitable to the subject, one taking the first verse, and the next the second, and so on. This they will do standing and facing the society. Of course the success of the plan depends upon the ingenuity of the leader of the club, and his power of arousing enthusiasm.

Progress Bands.— A very efficient scheme for bettering the prayer meeting is that of dividing the society into bands of perhaps six members each, calling them Progress Band A, Progress Band B, etc. In making the division see that each band has in it some person of considerable experience and ability in prayer-meeting work, at least one beginner, and others in all stages between. Make out a schedule for each band — how many persons it contains who have never led a meeting, never led in public prayer, given an original testimony, etc. Then the bands will go to work, each trying to see how great progress it can make. A committee of graduate members may watch the work and award the honors, if honors are in prospect. At any rate, if the leaders of the bands are enthusiastic, the society will get a capital awakening and some marked progress will be made.

Big Brothers and Big Sisters.— The Big Brother idea which has been applied so finely to city boys may be applied as well to our Christian Endeavor prayer meetings. Call a meeting of the older members of the society, both young men and young women, and set the plan before them. Ask them if they will not each of them take under their care some younger member of the society and help him or her in the prayer-meeting work and in the general work of the society, talking over the prayer-meeting topics, leading him on in more difficult ways of taking part, and seeking to develop his thoughtfulness and his Christian character. Present this as a real service to the King in the persons of His children, and then call for volunteers. Divide up the beginners of the society among these volunteers. No public notice is to be taken of the movement, though each of the beginners will be told of the plan by his Big Brother or Big Sister.

Cutting Out Their Work for Them.— The prayer-meeting committee may be of assistance to many beginners by setting before them a definite programme of progress. You may, for instance, go to a boy who has just joined the society and say to him, " You will be getting used to the sound of your voice at first and overcoming some natural diffidence by merely reading Bible verses, but we expect you as soon as possible to take advantage of the opportunity for training which the society offers you. Therefore we suggest that you follow this schedule." The list you will hand him may read like this: March 1 to April 1, read Bible verses; April 2 to May 1, repeat Bible verses from memory; May 2 to June 1, add a sentence of original comment to the Bible verse you repeat; June 2 to July 1, read a quotation from some secular writer, adding a word of your own; July 2 to August 1, join in the sentence prayers; August 2 to September 1, offer prayer by yourself; September 2 to October 1, give an original testimony; October 2, lead a meeting." Of course this schedule will be varied according to your knowledge of the boy, and it will be well to talk it over with him, making such changes in it as he suggests. By this means he will adopt it as his own. Keep a copy of it and give him a jog from time to time if he falls behind the schedule in his progress.

Prayer-Meeting "Lectures." — The prayer meeting should give opportunity for training in extended religious discourse as well as in the brief talks of the ordinary meeting. As an occasional prayer-meeting feature, why not appoint six members (or more) to give before the society a series of six "lectures" on subjects appropriate to the society, but not necessarily connected with the prayer-meeting topics? The "lectures" (one a week) should be strictly confined to fifteen minutes, and the opening exercises should be cut short for them, that the time of the members for participation may not be lessened. The lectures may deal with a series of Christian heroes, such as Livingstone, Gladstone, Henry Drummond, Florence Nightingale, John B. Gough, and John Howard. They may deal with six Christian doctrines, such as the atonement, the new birth, the punishment of sin, the rewards of goodness, the power of prayer, and immortality. They may deal with the fundamental principles of your denomination, or with the great boards of your denomination. Whatever subjects are taken, give ample time for preparation, and insist that the lectures shall be "talks" and not read from manuscript.

The Prayer-Meeting Press.— In order to get the beginners to do some original thinking on the prayer-meeting topics, you may occasionally throw the meeting into the form of a newspaper edited by one of the best readers and most active workers in the society. He will go about among the members soliciting contributions from all. These contributions are to be original thoughts on the prayer-meeting topic, carefully written out. The editor will try to get varied contributions, as all editors do, asking now for a Bible verse with a comment, now for a secular quotation with a comment, now for an experience bearing on the subject, now for an illustration, and perhaps asking some poetically inclined member for a bit of verse. These will all be read by the editor sympathetically and clearly, and now and then he will add a comment of his own. He will pause several times for singing and for sentence prayers. Sometimes it will be best to have two papers, on successive evenings, one edited by a young man and written by the males of the society, the other edited by a young woman and written by the females. One of these may be called *The Prayer-Meeting Herald,* and the other *The Prayer-Meeting Tribune.*

Month Leaders.— A small society may solve the

problem of getting leaders by appointing each for a month at a time. There are advantages in this long service as prayer-meeting leader, for it gives a training which cannot be obtained so well by single evenings now and then, and the leader, if he is a good one, can do more for the society in a succession of evenings than in a single meeting. Moreover, it is an excellent plan to couple with the month's leader a series of beginners as assistant leaders. They get as much training as they are ready for, and the meetings at the same time receive expert guidance.

Society Five Minutes.— It would not be at all inappropriate to spend five minutes in every prayer meeting, at least for a series of weeks, in discussing the work of some one committee or officer of the society. The chairman of the committee or the officer will have the floor, and will tell the society what is wanted from the members to help carry on the work of the committee or office. At the same time he will ask for suggestions, and will try to draw out the members who have work to propose. To start the ball to rolling he may ask some member to be ready, when the invitation comes, to rise and give some hint for his committee or office. The time for this exercise should be limited strictly to five minutes. Of course only one committee or one office will be considered at a meeting, and it will be announced a week in advance so that the members will do some thinking on the subject. This plan will be found to halt at first, perhaps; but the members will soon wake up to it, and each five minutes will be better than the period of the week before.

THE NEW ENDEAVOR LIBRARY

12 Books   18 Booklets   30 in All

BOOKS

Christian Endeavor Manual, The	$1.00
Intermediate Manual, The	.75
Expert Endeavor	.50
Junior Text-Book, The	.50
Pledge Promptings	.35
Citizens in Training	.35
Eighty Pleasant Evenings	.35
Fuel for Missionary Fires	.35
Missionary Manual, The	.35
Officers' Handbook, The	.35
Prayer-Meeting Methods	.35
Weapons for Temperance Warfare	.35

BOOKLETS

Christian Endeavor Grace-Notes	$0.10
Christian Endeavor Ink	.10
Christian Endeavor Unions	.10
Christian Endeavor Greeting, The	.10
On the Lookout	.10
Our Crowning Meeting	.10
Sunday-school Endeavors	.10
Quiet Hour, The	.10
Plans for the Missionary Committees	.08
Christian Endeavor in Principle and Practice	.05
Effective Temperance Committee	.05
Flower-Committee Summary	.05
Good-Literature Committee at Work	.05
Social Committee at Work	.05
Helps and Hints for Junior Workers	.05
Why and How of Junior Endeavor	.05
Social Service for Young People	.05
Tonic for the Timid	.05
	$6.88

Price Complete, $5.50 prepaid

NOTE. — Each book or booklet named in this library will be sold separately if desired, at the price quoted opposite the name, sent post-paid.

United Society of Christian Endeavor
BOSTON AND CHICAGO

CARDS

OUR FULL LINE
Per 100

Absentee Card...	$0.50
Active Member's Pledge. Nos. 1, 2, 3, or 4........	.50
Application-Cards....................................	.50
Associate Member's Pledge.........................	.50
Christian Endeavor Life-Work Recruit Cards....	.50
Decision-Cards.......................................	.50
Floating Society. Introduction-cards...............	.50
Floating Society. Pledge-cards.....................	.50
Floating Society. Report-Cards....................	.50
Flower Committee. Gilt edge.......................	.75
With name of society inserted..................	1.00
Honorary Member's Pledge.........................	.50
Intermediate Active Pledge........................	.50
Junior Committee Badges. 5 cents each; in lots of five; 3 cents each.	
Junior Daily Record of Bible-Reading............	.50
Junior Lookout-Committee Excuse-Card........	.30
Junior Membership Pledge........................	.50
Junior Missionary Offering........................	3.00
Junior Preparatory Pledge.........................	.30
Junior Temperance Pledge........................	.30
Junior Topic-Cards..................................	1.00
Lookout-Committee Reminder...................	.50
Monthly-Offering Pledge-Cards..................	.30
Mothers' Society Pledge...........................	.50
Prayer-Meeting Committee Reminder..........	.50
Prayer-Meeting Invitation. No. 1.................	.50
With name of society and time of meeting inserted	1.00
Prayer-Meeting Topic-Cards. Topics for one year from the month ordered........................	1.00
Quarterly Record-Cards. For the use of lookout committees...	.50
Quiet Hour Covenant-Card.......................	.50
Reciprocal Prayer-Cards...........................	.50
Sunday-school Committee Invitation...........	.30
Suggestions to Leaders............................	.50
Suggestions for the Lookout Committee. Set of five for 10 cents...................................	.03
Suggestions for the Missionary Committee. Set of five for 10 cents...................................	.03
Suggestions for the Prayer-Meeting Committee. Set of five for 10 cents............................	.03
Suggestions for the Social Committee. Set of five for 10 cents.......................................	.03
Suggestions for the Sunday-school Committee. Set of five for 10 cents................................	.03
Temperance Pledge-Cards.........................	.50
Treasurer's Cards...................................	.50

United Society of Christian Endeavor

BOSTON AND CHICAGO

HELPFUL BOOKS

Prayers for the Quiet Hour. By FLOYD W. TOMKINS, S.T.D., LL.D. 12 mo. Cloth-bound. Title in gold. Price $1.00, postpaid.

Dr. Tomkins is so well known to Christian Endeavorers that we need only to say that these prayers were contributed by him in connection with Christian Endeavor topics. It is the best devotional book yet published for the "Quiet Hour." We should like to see it placed in the hands of every Christian.

Happiness Haven. By AMOS R. WELLS. Bound in beautiful olive cloth with gold stamp and gold top. 80 pp. Price, 50 cents, postpaid.

This book contains two very helpful essays on happiness and Christ's way to it. In his delightful way Professor Wells gives in the first essay a bright, clear, and comprehensive view of the possibility of avoiding sinful worries, while in the second essay, entitled "The Beatitudes of To-day," we have his interpretation of the Beatitudes in their application to modern conditions. It is a happiness book, written in a happy vein, with the express purpose of helping others to be truly happy. A splendid gift-book.

A Treasure of Hymns. By AMOS R. WELLS. Cloth, gold-stamped. Price, $1.60, postpaid.

This is the sixtieth book published by this voluminous writer. In its 392 large pages he gives the history of 120 famous hymns and their writers, including accounts of striking scenes in which the hymns have played a part.

These hymns are all by different writers, including all the greatest hymn-writers of the English language, with others of second rank, so that the book constitutes a biographical dictionary of hymnody. For each of these 120 writers of noble hymns are given a biographical sketch, a list of his notable hymns, the accurate and full text of the hymn selected as his best, and anecdotes of the use of the hymn. Thus the book is sure to be an invaluable aid to ministers, prayer-meeting workers, Sunday-school workers, and in the home, as well as indeed a "treasure" to all lovers of our noble Christian hymns. It is handsomely printed and bound.

United Society of Christian Endeavor
BOSTON AND CHICAGO

HELPFUL BOOKS

Why We Believe the Bible. By AMOS R. WELLS. 167 pp. 12 mo. Cloth, gilt dies. Price, $1.00 postpaid.

The best book on Christian Evidences published in many years. Professor Wells has spent the greater part of his life in Bible study and exposition, and this valuable book is the rich result of almost a life-work. A splendid tonic for weak faith. We heartily commend this work to pastors, teachers, and young people that desire to enter into any kind of Christian work. It will also serve as an admirable text-book on Christian Evidences, the brisk question-and-answer form adopted by the writer peculiarly suiting it to this purpose.

The Young People's Pastor. By AMOS R. WELLS. 115 pp. Attractively bound in dark-green cloth, with gold lettering. Price, 75 cents, postpaid.

Young people's societies need the co-operation of the pastor, and the pastor needs the co-operation of the young people. Mr. Wells in twelve chapters shows how the pastor may utilize the help of his young people and set them to work. These chapters are as follows: "The Pastor in the Prayer Meeting," "The Pastor in the Business Meeting," "The Pastor over the Committees," "The Pastor in the Executive Committee," "The Pastor in the Socials," "The Pastor and the Junior Society," "The Pastor in the Union Meetings," "The Pastor as Utilizer," "The Pastor as Praiser," "The Pastor at the Brakes," "The Pastor and the Pledge," "The Pastor and the Society at Large." This book was written to emphasize the need of larger attention to the matter of training the church of the future, on the part of pastors and churches, and to indicate the lines along which labor may most profitably be directed.

Bible Chains. By AMOS R. WELLS. 76 pp. Cloth, 35 cents. Postpaid.

This selection of Bible verses was first put out in a pamphlet for the Juniors; but it was thought to be equally helpful for adults, and for their convenience it now appears as a very attractive cloth-bound book of 76 pages. It contains 300 of the most helpful verses in the Bible, arranged for committing to memory. They are grouped under 33 leading topics, such as temptation, sorrow, purity, contentment, patience, peace, labor — just the topics on which we need to store our memory.

United Society of Christian Endeavor
BOSTON AND CHICAGO

www.ingramcontent.com/pod-product-compliance
Lightning Source LLC
Chambersburg PA
CBHW031349040426
42444CB00005B/248